INHERITANCE
TAX
A PRACTICAL GUIDE
Second Edition

Stoy Hayward

**KOGAN
PAGE**

First published in 1986 by Kogan Page Ltd, 120 Pentonville Road, London N1 9JN.

Reprinted 1986

Second edition first published in 1989

Printed and bound in Great Britain by Biddles Ltd, Guildford and King's Lynn

British Library Cataloguing in Publication Data
Inheritance tax: a practical guide. - 2nd ed.
  1. Great Britain. Property. Inheritance.
  Taxation
  I. Stoy Hayward & Co. II. Stillerman,
  Barry. Inheritance tax.
  336.2′76

ISBN 1-85091-600-4

Contents

EXEMPTIONS AND RELIEFS

THE WAYS OF GIVING

ASSET SELECTION

THE FAMILY TRADING COMPANY

TAX-EFFICIENT INVESTMENTS

GIFTING ON DEATH

HUSBAND AND WIFE

THE NEED FOR INSURANCE

OVERSEAS PLANNING

CAPITAL GAINS TAX

PAYMENT AND ADMINISTRATION OF IHT

APPENDICES

INDEX

OTHER SERVICES OF THE FIRM

CURRENT PUBLICATIONS

UNITED KINGDOM OFFICES

INTERNATIONAL OFFICES

Preface

The abolition of capital transfer tax and its replacement with inheritance tax was one of the major surprises of the 1986 Budget statement. It required very careful reconsideration of the steps which could be taken to mitigate death duties. The radical changes to the tax regime which were announced in the 1988 Budget statement requires further analysis. The inheritance tax rates have now been simplified so that there is a nil rate band of £110,000 and a flat rate of 40% for all assets over £110,000. This replaces the progressive scale of rates and is good news for the wealthy who would have previously paid tax of up to 60%. The top rate of tax for income tax, capital gains tax and inheritance tax is now the same, i.e. 40% and this puts a different perspective on the interaction between these taxes.

We now have an extremely liberal inheritance tax regime with the tax rates at an historically low level. Following the last general election, the political situation looks to be relatively stable for the next few years. However inheritance tax may become a political football in the future and is likely to become a more onerous tax upon a change of government. This is now an ideal time to review your financial position and take advantage of the planning areas which currently exist so that if, for example, tax rates were to increase in the future, you will have taken action to mitigate the eventual liability using the numerous existing techniques.

The purpose of this book is to describe the new legislation, consider the method of reviewing your financial position and potential inheritance tax liability and examine the planning areas which are available to save inheritance tax. If you would like us to carry out a review and report on your inheritance tax position, please complete and return the questionnaire which is at the back of this book.

BARRY STILLERMAN
October 1988

This book is written as a general guide. As any course of action must depend upon your individual circumstances; you are recommended to obtain specific professional advice before you proceed.

Acknowledgement

Barry Stillerman would like to express his thanks to Roz Comley and her colleagues in the technical and training section of the tax department at Stoy Hayward whose assistance on this book was invaluable.

Introduction

The changing tax structure

Death duties and taxes on gifts have been in existence in various forms throughout the century. Up to 1974 estate duty was levied on gifts made on or within seven years of death. Capital transfer tax (CTT) then replaced estate duty and levied tax on gifts during the donor's lifetime and at death. The rate of tax on lifetime transfers was one half of the rate applicable at death or within three years of death. With effect from 18 March 1986 the structure of gifts tax was again radically reformed. The abolition of the tax charge on lifetime transfers to individuals and certain trusts has meant that the structure of gifts tax has turned full circle and reverted back to a combination of estate duty and capital transfer tax. Indeed, certain aspects of inheritance tax may depend upon court decisions and Inland Revenue practice which applied under the estate duty rules.

As a charge will mainly arise on death it is really a tax on your dependants in respect of the wealth which passes to them and so CTT was renamed Inheritance Tax (IHT). The planning opportunities under IHT will be of interest if you wish to maximise the wealth you will be passing on or if you are a potential beneficiary who wishes to ensure that wealth is passed to you in the most tax-efficient way. Although the absence of any tax on lifetime gifts might lead to a rush to transfer wealth, the practical implications of such action should be carefully borne in mind. These are considered in the next section of this book.

The rates of tax

On death it is necessary to value your estate. Assets passing to your spouse are not charged until he or she dies but the passing of wealth to the other members of your family, for example your children, grandchildren, brothers and sisters, will give rise to a tax charge on the value of the wealth which is being transferred at that time. The examples in this book have been based on the 1988/89 flat rate of 40% for wealth of over £110,000. Prior to this year there was a complex and progressive scale of rates.

Taxable estates

As you will see from Appendix 1, tax applies to estates of over £110,000. This is a relatively low threshold and this will mean that many estates will be caught. For example a young married couple with the following wealth could have an estate which would be liable to IHT.

	£000
Value of house and contents (mortgage repaid by endowment policy)	95
Building society deposits	5
Car	5
Insurance policy payable to wife on first death	70
Total estate	175
Potential IHT	26

The incidence of IHT on death can be extremely penal. The following illustration shows the tax payable on chargeable estates of various sizes.

Value of chargeable estate	IHT payable
£000	£
100	nil
150	16,000
200	36,000
250	56,000
300	76,000
350	96,000
400	116,000
500	156,000
750	256,000
1,000	356,000

The taxation climate

The taxation climate has changed dramatically over the last few years. The House of Lords' judgements in the 1984 case Furniss-v-Dawson and the earlier cases of IRC-v-Burmah Oil Co Ltd and WT Ramsay-v-IRC have had a major impact on the anti-avoidance industry. These cases are now being relied upon by the Inland Revenue to enable steps inserted in a pre- ordained series of transactions, with no commercial or business purpose apart from the avoidance of tax, to be ignored even if the transactions were intended to achieve a legitimate commercial end. However, three recent cases including Craven-v-White were decided in the taxpayer's favour and have limited the application of these principles. In addition to the above cases, the inheritance tax legislation has its own anti-avoidance section entitled 'Associated Operations' which is widely drafted to catch direct and indirect transactions.

The fact that the very artificial schemes have been dealt a major blow means that commercial tax planning has become even more important especially in view of the Craven-v-White decision. Also the arrangements which allowed you to 'have your cake and eat it' by gifting while still retaining some control over the assets are to be unfavourably treated under the gifts with reservation rules. These changes mean that a fresh approach is required to estate planning which should be led by commercial rather than purely tax motives. However it is important to be aware of all the opportunities which are available as substantial savings can be made.

Prior to 1986 there were numerous up-front charges which may have prevented you from making a gift to your dependants. A capital gains tax charge may have arisen, stamp duty was levied on gifts and CTT may have become payable on the lifetime transfer. Now it is possible to make a gift during your lifetime without incurring any of these liabilities and this should greatly encourage estate planning.

The problem which was often encountered under the CTT regime as well as under estate duty was that planning was left too late. In theory, IHT can be avoided altogether by gifting all your assets now provided you survive seven years. Because of this, IHT is being called a voluntary tax. However, in practice this is not the case as very few people would be willing to jeopardise their financial security merely to avoid IHT. Such action could result in a reliance upon your family to provide for your future financial needs and this must be regarded as a dangerous situation. Estate planning will accordingly need to balance the retention of wealth to provide for future living expenses and contingencies, with the need to transfer wealth to your family as early as possible. In view of the complexity of inheritance tax, professional advice should be sought before undertaking an estate planning exercise.

The political climate

The present government appears to be sufficiently stable to continue through to the early 1990s before the next election which is due by 1993. However, a change of government could well result in a radical re-structuring of the tax regime so as to reduce estate planning opportunities.

The Labour Party introduced CTT in 1975 as a means of taxing transfers during lifetime and at death. It was proposed that this would bring about a 'substantial reduction in the massive amounts of inherited wealth concentrated in the hands of a tiny section of the population'. Under the Conservative Party, the top rate of tax on lifetime transfers has been reduced from 75% to 40% (and now under IHT can be avoided altogether), business and agricultural property reliefs were extended and the non-aggregation of transfers after ten (now seven) years was introduced. The Labour Party has stated that if it is to 'return to the original purposes of CTT, as a tax which can bring about a very real, if gradual, change in the present huge inequalities of personal wealth, it will be essential for most of the above concessions to be reversed'.

Since the 1960s, the Labour Party has been committed to the introduction of an annual Wealth Tax. An idea of how such a tax could work was published in 1977, the main features of which were as follows:

1) the tax should apply to those with assessed net wealth of over £100,000 (£213,000 in 1988 prices);

2) the rates would range from 1% on the first slice up to £300,000 to 5% on the slice over £5m (approximately £700,000 to £11m in 1988 prices);

3) there would be no exemption for owner-occupied housing but relief for small businesses and working farmers;

4) the wealth of husband and wife would be aggregated.

If, as part of an inheritance tax planning arrangement, wealth is gifted to children or grandchildren this could conceivably reduce the impact of wealth tax should it ever be introduced.

The SDP (now known as The Democrats) set out their proposals for capital taxation in 1985 in the Green Paper entitled 'Fairness and Enterprise'. This stated that 'the accumulation of hereditary wealth in the hands of a small proportion of the population is socially divisive and economically inefficient' — a similar view to that expressed by the Labour Party. The paper suggested a 'beefed-up CTT' rather than the introduction of a wealth tax. The proposals to make CTT a more effective tax were:

1) gifts should be aggregated throughout lifetime and on death (not just in the last seven years);

2) tax would be charged on lifetime gifts but up to a maximum figure;

3) the tax rates would be broadened to start at a lower level of 10% and increase to 70%;

4) the existing business and agricultural property reliefs would be restricted.

While these papers were written some years ago it is understood that these views are generally held today and give a guide to the likely position should there be a change of government. IHT is likely to become a political football in the future and its present structure very short-lived upon a change of government. Measures should be taken now to mitigate tax while the opportunity exists.

The practical considerations

Philosophy

Perhaps the most important consideration is whether, in fact, you want to give away any of your assets during your lifetime. The potential IHT savings from an estate planning exercise could be enormous but unless you want to pass wealth to your dependants there is no point in proceeding any further with a financial review. Of course, the assets need not be passed during your lifetime. Estate planning could be undertaken now so that wealth can be gifted efficiently on your death.

Your family relationships will also need to be considered. A man with an unstable marriage may appreciate the tax benefits of passing wealth equivalent to the nil rate band (currently £110,000) but may not wish to give wealth to his wife if it is likely that they will be divorced. You may have a very good relationship with your children at this time but will this still be so in, say, ten years? Gifting directly to minor children may be unwise as they may change dramatically during adolescence; if they are to receive funds at an early age they may squander the money or become less independent. Many self-made millionaires attribute part of the reason for their success to a lack of money in their formative years.

Current capital position

Having decided that you wish to take some measures to reduce the impace of IHT on your estate, the next step is to establish your present capital position. This means valuing all your assets (including your pension fund, life policies and assets which are held in trust for you or your wife) and quantifying your liabilities. A simplified example of a capital and income summary is set out in Appendix 2. From this list a capital statement can be compiled as shown in Appendix 3. This will show the total value of your estate and the assets which could be gifted.

Having considered your capital position, it will then be possible to compute the likely IHT liability based on the current value of your estate. This calculation will need to take account of the way in which the estate is to be distributed on death. Also the financial position may change on death with, for example, the house mortgage being repaid out of the proceeds of an endowment policy. A computation based on the details shown in Appendices 2 and 3 is set out in Appendix 4.

Current income position

Having reviewed your current capital position and the likely IHT charge it is then necessary to examine your current income position and financial needs. The sources of capital are set out in the questionnaire and the level of income from these sources will need to be listed, as shown in Appendix 2. This information can then be transferred to an estimated net spendable income schedule which is illustrated in Appendix 5. This schedule highlights three figures:

1) your tax liability;

2) your net income after tax; and

3) your net income after living expenses.

Appendix 5 shows that based on the assumptions in the illustration there is net income after all these items. The annual expenditure of £35,000 will include private expenses, a list of which is set out in Appendix 6.

If the net spendable income schedule shows that the expenditure exceeds net income then you are living off your capital and it may be necessary to gift non-income producing assets to ensure that your net income is not reduced. It may also be necessary to review your financial position and examine whether you are maximising your after-tax income and capital return from your investments. If there is net income after expenditure, then income-producing assets could be gifted without adversely prejudicing your financial position.

Future income requirements

So far only your current requirements have been considered, but if assets are to be gifted permanently it will be necessary to ensure that you have sufficient wealth to meet your future living expenditure and any contingencies. Sometimes elderly people who only need a low income are reluctant to part with wealth in case it is required to meet large medical and nursing bills.

Your current income position could change dramatically in the future, for example, on retirement. Normally your earnings will fall, for although you may become entitled to state benefits, your salary or remuneration will no longer be paid. However the loss of income on retirement may be mitigated by a good pension scheme and by rearranging your investments. For example, because of your current tax position your funds may be invested in capital producing assets such as gilts which could be switched to high income investments on retirement. You may not need such a large house on retirement. Moving to a smaller house should release capital which could be invested.

On your death your wife, if she does not work, will be reliant upon any pension and income from the assets which are left to her to provide for her future needs. The example in Appendix 7 shows that based on certain assumptions, there should be sufficient income if the funds are reinvested in high yielding deposits so that assets could be gifted without adversely affecting likely future income needs. However, each case will need to be considered separately. A similar computation based on other facts may paint a very different picture.

Stoy Hayward

A member of Horwath & Horwath International

Stoy Hayward Inheritance Tax Questionnaire

Please complete and return to:

Barry Stillerman

Stoy Hayward

8 Baker Street,

London,

W1M 1DA.

Stoy Hayward
8 Baker Street, London W1M 1DA (01-486-5888)

Inheritance tax questionnaire   (Inheritance tax contact: Barry Stillerman)

The book describes the method of reviewing your financial position, computing your potential inheritance tax liability and the planning areas which are available to save inheritance tax. If you would like us to carry out a review and report on your inheritance tax position then please complete and return this questionnaire.

1. Personal details

    Name (Self):   (Wife):

    Address:

    Date of birth:

    Occupation:

    Telephone no. (Home):   (Office):

2. Family details

Full names of children	Date of birth	Occupation	Tick if married	Ages of grandchildren

3. Previous gifts within last 7 years

Date	Donor Self/spouse	Beneficiary	Asset given	Value

    Please include details of assets transferred into a settlement and provide a copy of the trust deed.

4. Capital and income summary

	Capital		Gross income	
	Self	Spouse	Self	Spouse
	£000	£000	£	£

Assets

Private residence ....
Contents ....
Other property...
Agricultural land/woodlands..........................
Chattels, jewellery ....
Shares in your trading company...................
Other business assets ....
Shares in other private companies..............
Bank deposit accounts ....
Bank current accounts ....
Building society deposits ....
Shares in quoted companies..........................
Gilts and other securities..............................
National savings, premium bonds.................
Trust funds..
Lloyds funds (deposits and reserves)..........
Other assets, loans...

Earned income ....
Benefits ....

Liabilities   Interest payable

Mortgage on home ....
Other property loans ....
Bank loans and overdrafts.............................
Tax and other liabilities.................................

Value of pension schemes

5. Life policies	First policy	Second policy	Third policy

5. Life policies

Life assured:

Beneficiary of policy:

Type of policy:

Annual premium: £

　　　　　　　　Payer

Sum assured:

Current value:

Date of policy:

Name of company:

---

6. Any other relevant information

Please attach a copy of your latest wills or summarise their terms:

Please indicate any likely future change in your financial position, e.g. retirement:

Please confirm that you and your wife are domiciled in the UK:

Please indicate any likely future inheritance:

Any other relevant information:

The basic rules

On death

As mentioned earlier, your estate is valued on death and the assets passing to your spouse are excluded from the calculation of the IHT due. If you refer to the example which is set out in Appendices 2 to 7 and assume that the following assets are left to the children with the balance to the spouse then the tax charge will be as set out below.

Chargeable transfers	£
Investment property	80,000
Less Loan	(40,000)
	40,000
Shares in quoted companies	50,000
Bank and building society deposits	40,000
Chargeable transfer	£130,000
IHT — on first £110,000	nil
20,000 × 40%	8,000
130,000	£8,000

Relief may be claimed if certain qualifying investments (such as quoted shares) are sold within one year after death or property is sold within three years after death at a value which is lower than the probate value. In these cases the sale price may be taken instead of the probate value.

Successive charges

There are relieving provisions which apply if wealth is received and then passed on within five years. These rules, which can be easily overlooked, are designed to avoid IHT being levied twice on the same assets within a five year period. The tax relief is the relevant percentage, as set out below, of the tax charged on the value of the original transfer which again becomes subject to IHT.

Period of time between first and second transfer	Relevant percentage %
0–1 year	100
1–2 years	80
2–3 years	60
3–4 years	40
4–5 years	20
over 5 years	Nil

An individual has a chargeable estate of £500,000. On death, this estate includes an asset worth £150,000 which was valued at £100,000 two and a half years earlier when it was left to him by his father. On his father's death IHT of £40,000 was paid on the asset.

	£
IHT on chargeable estate of £500,000	156,000
Less Relief £40,000 × 60%	(24,000)
IHT payable	£132,000

This relief could be lost if on the second death, no charge arises possibly because the estate is left to the spouse. In such cases it may be advisable to gift the asset to say the children and pass other wealth to the spouse.

Lifetime gifts

There is no charge on the following lifetime gifts by individuals so long as the gift is made more than seven years before death:

—gifts to individuals
—gifts into an accumulation and maintenance trust
—gifts into a life interest trust
—gifts into a trust for the disabled

A lifetime gift by an individual into a discretionary trust is charged at half the rate which is applicable on death. If the donor pays the tax then the gift will need to be grossed up. The grossing up rates are set out in Appendix 1. It has been assumed for the purpose of the examples in this book that the donee pays the tax.

An individual transfers £120,000 to a discretionary trust and has made no other gifts in the last seven years.

	£
Chargeable transfer	120,000
IHT thereon—on £110,000	Nil
10,000 × 40%	4,000
120,000	4,000
Lifetime tax charge £4,000 × 50%	£2,000

Gifts made within seven years of death

Although a transfer may appear to be tax-free (for example lifetime gifts between individuals) it may be caught if the donor dies within seven years of making the gift. For this reason such gifts are known as potentially exempt transfers and they become exempt after seven years. The IHT rates and bands which are applied to a gift made within seven years of death will be those in force on the death of the donor. The transfer will then be taxed on its value at the time of making the gift and not on its value on death. However, if the value of the asset gifted has fallen, relief can be claimed by calculating the tax due using the market value of the asset at the date of death rather than its value when gifted. Tapering relief will be available if the gift was made more than three years before death as follows.

Years between death and gift	Tapering relief
	%
0–3	Nil
3–4	20
4–5	40
5–6	60
6–7	80

An individual gifts an asset worth £120,000 (£150,000 on death) to his son four and a half years before death.

	£
Chargeable gift	120,000
IHT thereon on £110,000	Nil
10,000 × 40%	4,000
120,000	4,000
Less Tapering relief at 40%	1,600
IHT payable	£2,400

If a chargeable transfer (for example a gift to a discretionary trust) is made within seven years of death. IHT may have been paid at half the full rate when the gift was made. It will be necessary to recompute the tax charge using the rates, bands and tapering relief in force at the date of death and deduct any tax originally paid. If the tax computed on the gift at death is less than the tax originally paid, no repayment will be made.

An individual gifts £120,000 to a discretionary trust three and a half years before death and leaves all his wealth to his spouse on death.

IHT payable on gift £4,000 × 50%	£2,000

Further IHT payable on death (assuming no change in the IHT rates and bands).

	£
Tax at full rates on death	4,000
Less Tapering relief at 20%	(800)
	3,200
Less Tax originally paid	(2,000)
Tax payable	£1,200

Cumulation period

The rate of tax which is applied to a chargeable transfer depends on whether any gifts have been made in the preceding seven years. Gifts are taxed in chronological order. If the nil rate band has been used up by earlier gifts, it will not be available for gifts which are made in the next seven years so that the later gifts will be taxable.

An individual transfers £120,000 to a discretionary trust and a further £60,000 is settled four years later. The tax payable (assuming that he survives a further seven years) will be:

		£	£
First transfer	£110,000	Nil	
	10,000 × 40%	4,000	
	120,000	4,000	
Lifetime tax charge	£4,000 × 50%		2,000
Second transfer	£60,000 × 40%	24,000	
Lifetime tax charge	£24,000 × 50%		12,000
Total tax payable			£14,000

When computing any IHT payable on assets in a discretionary trust, regard must be had to chargeable transfers made by the settlor within the period of seven years before the settlement was created.

After seven years chargeable transfers are 'written-off' for IHT purposes and are not taken into account when considering the rate of tax applicable on any future gifts. In the above example if the second settlement of £60,000 had been made more than seven years after the first transfer, the tax charge of £12,000 would have been avoided as the £60,000 transfer would have been covered by the nil rate band.

The additional tax payable if a gift is caught within the seven year period before death can be substantial as the chargeable transfer is also taken into account when computing the tax payable on the estate at death.

Debts

Special provisions apply to debts owed at the date of death. Normally such debts can be deducted from the value of the estate when computing IHT. However if the debt was not bona fide incurred for full consideration by the deceased for his own use and benefit then it may not be deducted. Therefore if the deceased had taken out a mortgage to buy his home, that debt would have been 'incurred bona fide for full consideration' and should be deductible but if the asset acquired was not enjoyed by the deceased the debt would not be deductible. For example, if an individual buys an asset in his son's name and incurs a loan in doing so, the loan will not be an allowable deduction from his estate as it was incurred for his son's (and not his own) benefit. Special provisions apply to deny the deduction of a debt incurred in connection with a life insurance policy if the sum assured does not form part of that person's estate.

An individual gifts £120,000 to his son four and a half years before death. If the chargeable estate on death is £350,000 then the tax position will be:

	£	£
Tax on gift of £120,000		2,400
Tax on estate at death £350,000 × 40%		140,000
Total tax payable		142,400

Tax charge if a gift made more than seven years before death

		£
Tax on lifetime gift of £120,000		2,400
Tax on estate of £350,000 at death	£100,000 Nil	
	240,000 × 40% 96,000	
	350,000	
		98,400
Additional tax arising on death		£44,000

The provisions can also apply if the deceased made a gift, say to his son, and then borrowed money back from his son. The gift may be exempt if it was made more than seven years before his death but the debt will not be an allowable deduction. If the loan is later repaid it will be treated as a potentially exempt transfer which becomes exempt seven years later.

Gifts with reservation

Generally

While the abolition of IHT on certain gifts made more than seven years before death will help estate planning, especially for the wealthy, the rules dealing with 'gifts with reservation' (which have been revived from the estate duty legislation) will in many cases make estate planning a more painful exercise.

An individual may be happy to gift his home so long as he and his wife are able to continue living there for the rest of their lives. He may wish to gift other assets to save tax but not wish to lose total control over them. The individual being prudent may wish to ensure that he is protected should his financial position worsen, in which case he may want to receive back part of the wealth he originally gifted. Under CTT this requirement could be met by the donor and his wife becoming trustees and potential beneficiaries under a trust so that they could, in the future, exercise their discretion as trustees and appoint capital to themselves as beneficiaries. This arrangement was often included in the CTT inheritance trust schemes.

The philosophy behind IHT is that if a gift is to be made, it should be made outright. The gifts with reservation rules extend this general principle and catch arrangements which are designed to enable a donor to 'have his cake and eat it'. These rules have been in place since the introduction of IHT in 1986, but the interpretation of a 'gift with reservation' is still not clear. Lifetime gifts do not have to be reported to the Inland Revenue, so they will not say whether they think there is any reservation of benefit. A decision would be made if the individual died within seven years, so that the lifetime gift was taxable. By this time, of course, it would be too late to revise any unsuccessful tax planning.

The rules

The legislation states that the gifts with reservation rules will apply 'if an individual makes a gift and either

a)   possession and enjoyment of the property is not bona fide assumed by the donee at or before the beginning of the relevant period; or

b)   at any time in the relevant period the property is not enjoyed to the entire exclusion or virtually to the entire exclusion, of the donor and of any benefit to him by contract or otherwise, ...'

It should be noted that the position of both the donee and the donor must be considered. As the relevant period is the seven years before death the provisions can apply even if the donor gifts an asset outright but obtains an interest in it at some time in the future. Exempt gifts such as inter-spouse transfers will not be caught by the rules.

The effect of a gift with reservation

If a gift is caught by the provisions, the asset gifted is still deemed to be beneficially owned by the donor. This means that its value will form part of the donor's estate for IHT purposes if no action is taken. An IHT charge could arise when the gift is made if, for example, the asset is settled into a discretionary trust. In this case tax may be paid on making the gift and the asset will still form part of the donor's estate.

If action is taken by the donor at some future stage so that he no longer has any interest in the asset, then it will no longer form part of his estate. By renouncing his interest, he will be making a gift based on the value of the asset at that time and if the donor survives seven years, the gift will become exempt.

Therefore if the gift was originally made to another individual and the reservation of interest is waived more than seven years before death IHT can still be avoided. The position on death is as follows:

Event	Tax charge
If the reservation was released more than seven years before death	— no charge
If the reservation was released within seven years of death	— charge on value of gift when reservation released less any tax payable on the original gift
If the reservation was not released until death	— gift taxed as part of the estate at its value on death less any tax payable on the original gift

Property

There are two situations where a donor may gift property with a reservation of interest without the above rules applying. These exceptions are as follows:

1) in the case of land or a chattel which is enjoyed by the donor if full consideration (i.e. a full market rent) is paid; or

2) if an occupation of the property
(a) results from a change in the circumstances of the donor since making the gift which was unforeseen when the gift was made, and
(b) occurs when the donor has become unable to maintain himself through old age, infirmity or otherwise, and
(c) it represents a reasonable provision by the donee for the care and maintenance of the donor, and
(d) the donee is a relative of the donor or his spouse.

An individual gifts an asset worth £120,000 to a discretionary trust in which he retains an interest. He dies eight years later when his estate is worth £600,000 and the value of the trust's asset has grown to £500,000.

	Value of estate for IHT purposes	IHT
	£	£
Value of estate on death	600,000	
Add Value of trust's asset	500,000	
Chargeable estate for IHT	1,100,000	396,000
Less tax paid on original gift of £120,000		4,000
Tax payable on death		£392,000

An individual who has an estate of £600,000 gifts his house worth £200,000 to his son and pays a market rent of, say, £16,000 p.a. so that a gift with reservation is not made. He dies eight years later when the house is worth £350,000.

	£	£
Donor		
Annual payment of rent £16,000 × 8		128,000
Donee		
Annual receipt of rent	16,000	
Less Income tax thereon (say)	(4,000)	
Annual receipt	12,000	
Total net receipts £12,000 × 8		96,000
Value of house on death of donor	350,000	
IHT saving at 40%	140,000	
Potential CGT on house after indexation allowance (say)	(25,000)	
		115,000
		£211,000

These exceptions are unlikely to be of great assistance. The first one involves the payment of a full market rent for the property. The rent would need to be funded by the donor each year and would be taxable on the donee. The second exclusion would appear to apply in fairly limited circumstances, for example, if a relative receives property from the donor and subsequently needs to look after the donor. However, there still remains scope for passing property to children provided the transactions are considered at an early stage.

Anti-avoidance

The gifts with reservation rules are both complex and widely drafted. They are likely to prove to be one of the most difficult areas for individuals who wish to gift without losing control. They are also likely to become one of the main areas in which avoidance arrangements will be devised. Undoubtedly many of them will be challenged by the Inland Revenue. Therefore in planning, full regard must be had to the anti-avoidance cases of Furniss-v-Dawson and Ramsay-v-IRC or the associated operations provisions. However the recent Craven-v-White decision may be of some assistance.

Provisions exist so that if the asset (other than money) changes hands after the gift, the Inland Revenue can substitute the replaced property for the original asset which is gifted subject to reservation. Special 'see through' provisions also apply to settled property gifted with reservation. Further provisions exist to catch a gift in connection with an insurance policy on the life of the donor or his spouse if the benefits which accrue to the donee vary in accordance with the benefits enjoyed by the donor or his spouse.

The spouse

The gifts with reservation rules clearly catch a reservation to the donor, but do not deal with a reservation to the donor's spouse. In the Parliamentary Standing Committee debate Mr Brooke, for the Government, said, '... In general, and subject to what I shall say about insurance-based schemes, we take the view that when a person gives away a property with a reservation for his spouse and then shares the spouse's enjoyment or benefit of the reservation without paying for it, he cannot be said to be excluded from enjoyment or benefit of the gifted property ...'

It would appear that under certain circumstances, the reservation to the spouse may provide the donor with the comfort he seeks while not resulting in the gifts with reservation rules applying. However, the inclusion of the spouse in a class of beneficiaries under a discretionary trust could lead to adverse income tax implications which will need to be borne in mind.

Estate duty cases

As the gifts with reservation rules applied to estate duty, certain estate duty cases are likely to apply to transactions which are carried out under the IHT regime. Appendix 8 sets out a brief summary of some of the leading cases.

The Permanent Trustee Co, Worral, Cochrane and Earl Grey cases which are explained in Appendix 8, show that there is significant case law to support the gifts with reservation rules. The Oakes case may need to be borne in mind if shares in the family trading company are to be gifted. The Perpetual Trustee case is helpful in showing that a settlor can be a trustee without falling foul of the gifts with reservation rules.

Carving out an interest

The Munro estate duty case (see Appendix 8) is of particular interest. It held that if an interest was 'carved out' before the gift was made then the gifts with reservation rules could be avoided in respect of the entire property. This approach can be useful when considering the family home, often the most valuable asset in the estate.

A 75 year old grants a 20 year lease of his house to a nominee for himself and his wife and then gifts the freehold reversion to his daughter. He dies after 13 years when the house is worth £450,000, the value of the freehold reversion is, say, £275,000 and the value of the lease, say £150,000.

	£	£
IHT on death, assuming entire value of house comprised in the estate		
£110,000		Nil
340,000 × 40%		136,000
£450,000		136,000
IHT on lease		
£110,000	Nil	
40,000 × 40%	16,000	
150,000		
		16,000
IHT saving		£120,000

The principle is that the retained lease is not a gift, and therefore not a reservation of benefit. Moreover, it would not be necessary to pay a realistic market value rent. The inheritance tax benefits depend upon the value of the lease which is retained in the estate at death being relatively low and the freehold reversion having been gifted at least seven years before death. (The lease cannot be a lease for life as that would constitute a settlement.)

The other tax implications must be carefully borne in mind in any transaction of this nature. The holders of the freehold reversion are unlikely to obtain any benefit from the main residence or dependent relative exemptions as the occupiers would be enjoying their occupation by virtue of the leasehold interest. The eventual capital gains tax could be high because of the relatively low base value at the time of the gift. There could be an income tax disadvantage relating to lease premiums of the property were sold while the lease was still in force. There is also a possibility that the Inland Revenue might apply the associated operation rules.

The sequence of events is important as shown by the Nichols and Chick cases (see Appendix 8). These clearly show that any 'carve out' which takes place at the time of, or after, the gift should be caught by the gifts with reservation provisions.

A large part of the capital gains tax charge could be deferred by putting the freehold reversion into a UK trust and exporting the trust in the tax year before the freehold is sold. However, at the time of publication of this book, it is understood that such action is likely to be covered in the wide review of the taxation treatment of offshore trusts. Such action may not be effective if the legislation changes to catch this planning device. The law governing this aspect of tax planning is complex, and professional advice should be taken.

Further clarification

Clearly the gifts with reservation provisions will continue to create problems for taxpayers and their advisors in deciding whether they are likely to be applied to a particular transaction or series of transactions. A letter dated 18 May 1987 from Mr BT Houghton of the Inland Revenue to Mr MP Cornwell-Kelly of The Law Society was published in The Law Society's Gazette issue of 1 June 1988. It is particularly helpful in clarifying a number of matters and is accordingly reproduced below.

'Following our discussions on the inheritance tax matters raised in the Society's reform memorandum I am now able to write to you about the points concerning the provisions on gifts with reservation (GWR).

As we previously explained, it does not seem realistic to think in terms of precise and comprehensive guidance on how the GWR provisions will be interpreted and applied since so much will turn on the particular facts of individual cases. However, as the provisions are similar to those adopted for Estate Duty, the relevant Estate Duty case law and practice provide a helpful guide to the interpretation and application of the inheritance tax legislation. That said, may I turn to your specific concerns.

Gifts of land

1. Consistent with the assurance given (in 1986) by the Minister of State in Standing Committee G (Hansard, 10 June 1986, col 425), the Estate Duty practice on the treatment of gifts involved a share in a house where the gifted property is occupied by all the joint owners including the donor will apply. The donor's retention of a share in the property will not, by itself, amount to a reservation. If, and for so long as, all the joint owners remain in occupation, the donor's occupation will not be treated as a reservation provided the gift is

itself unconditional and there is no collateral benefit to the donor. The payment by the donee of the donor's share of the running costs, for example, might be such a benefit. An arrangement will not necessarily be jeopardised merely because it involves a gift of an unequal share in a house.

2. In other cases the donor's occupation or enjoyment of the gifted land will only be disregarded if the occupaton is for full consideration in money or money's worth as provided in paragraph 6(1)(a) of schedule 20 to the Finance Act 1986 (or if it is by way of a reasonable 'care maintenance' provision within paragraph 6(1)(b). Whether an arrangement is for full consideration will of course depend on the precise facts. But among the attributes of an acceptable arrangement would be the existence of a bargain negotiated at arm's length by parties who were independently advised and which followed the normal commercial criteria in force at the time it was negotiated.

3. You raised the possibility that a donor might give his house subject to a prior lease created in his own favour. Consistent with the principles established in the case of Munro-v-Commissioners of Stamp Duties (New South Wales) (1934) AC 61, we would not normally expect the donor's retention of the lease to constitute a reservation, assuming that the creation of the lease and the subsequent gift of the property subject to that lease are independent transactions. We will, however, scrutinise carefully the application of the Munro principles where the leasehold interest was granted in connection with the gift of the freehold. The application or otherwise of the decision in Re Nichols (1975) 1 WLR 534 concerning a (donee) landlord's covenants would be a matter for determination in the light of all the relevant facts at the time of the donor's death.

Gifts involving family businesses or farms

4. A gift involving a family business or farm will not necessarily amount to a GWR merely because the donor remains in the business, perhaps as a director or a partner. For example, where the gift is of shares in a company, the continuation of reasonable commercial arrangements in the form of remuneration for the donor's ongoing services to the company entered into before the gift will not of itself amount to a reservation provided the remuneration is in no way linked to or beneficially affected by the gift. Similar considerations will apply in the case where the gift is into trust which empowered a trustee, who may be the donor, to retain director's fees etc, for his own benefit.

5. The Munro principle will also be relevant in determining the tax treatment of gifts affecting family farms where the donor and the donee continue to farm the land in pursuance of arrangements entered into prior to and independently of the gift. In cases where this principle does not apply the test of 'full consideration' for the purposes of paragraph 6(1)(a) will need to be satisfied with regard to the donor's occupation of the land. In applying that test we shall take account of all the circumstances surrounding the arrangement including the sharing of profits and losses, the donor's and the donee's interests in the land, and their respective commitment and expertise.

Gifts of chattels

6. You referred to potential difficulties in determining what amounts to 'full consideration' for the donor's continued enjoyment of gifted chattels, particularly pictures and paintings, for the purposes of paragraph 6 of schedule 20. These may not be insuperable, as appears from the recent case of Commissioners of Inland Revenue-v-MacPherson, and in any event it would be difficult to overturn an arm's length, commercial arrangement entered into by parties who were independently advised.

Settlor's retention of reversion

7. In the case where a gift is made into trust, the retention by the settlor (donor) of a reversionary interest under the trust is not considered to constitute a reservation, whether the retained interest arises under the express terms of the trust or it arises by operation of general law, for example, a resulting trust.'

Other matters which have also been clarified are as follows:

1. A transfers assets into a discretionary settlement. The class of beneficiaries includes A's wife at the trustees' discretion on a regular basis.

   The mere fact that the donor's spouse is a member of the class of potential beneficiaries should not suffice to bring the gift within the GWR provisions. However, the provisions relating to associated operations and certain life assurance arrangements need to be borne in mind.

2. The inclusion of the settlor among the class of beneficiaries subject to powers contained in his trust is considered to be sufficient to constitute his gift as a gift with reservation. Where there is a possibility of the settlor becoming included in the class of beneficiaries by exercise of a power in the settlement, it is considered likely that this would again constitute a gift with reservation.

3. The mere fact that a settlor is a trustee of an accumulation and maintenance settlement for his children would not of itself involve a reservation to him.

Exemptions and reliefs

Lifetime gifts

As mentioned previously lifetime gifts to individuals, interest in possession trusts, and accumulation and maintenance trusts are exempt from tax if the donor survives for seven years. This should greatly encourage individuals to gift assets to their dependants as the lifetime gift will reduce the chargeable estate on death. An illustration of the IHT savings which can be achieved (ignoring any future increase in the value of the asset gifted) is set out in Appendix 9.

The spouse

Transfers between husband and wife are not taxable during lifetime or on death. However, if a UK domiciled person transfers funds to his spouse who is not domiciled in the UK, only the first £55,000 of the transfer will be exempt, the excess will be chargeable. (This rule may be effected by any change of legislation following the recently published consultative document on the taxation treatment of overseas persons.) Both husband and wife have separate IHT bands, therefore savings can be made by ensuring that the nil rate band is utilised on each death.

As lifetime gifts between individuals are exempt if they are made more than seven years before death, the ages and health of the husband and wife should be taken into account when deciding who should make the gift. If for example a wife's life expectancy is greater than that of her husband, who owns the asset to be gifted, an inter-spouse transfer may be advisable so that the wife gifts the asset. If the gift is made on condition that the wife gifts it on, then the Ramsay doctrine and the associated operations provisions are likely to apply. However, if the gift is made unconditionally then it may be exempt.

The nil rate band

The first £110,000 of chargeable transfers are subject to a nil rate of tax. The IHT bands are index-linked so that they are likely to increase by a few thousand pounds each year. As gifts are 'written off' after seven years, a chargeable gift of £110,000 can be made by say settling funds in a discretionary trust and after seven years the index-equivalent of £110,000 can again be settled without giving rise to any tax charge. Therefore a husband and wife could make total chargeable transfers of at least £440,000 over a period of just over seven years without incurring a tax charge as these gifts would be covered by the nil rate band. If the assets gifted attracted 50% business property relief, the total chargeable transfers could amount to £880,000.

The annual exemption

The annual exemption of £3,000 applies to lifetime chargeable gifts made by the donor each year. A husband and wife each have separate annual exemptions of £3,000. If the annual exemption has not been fully utilised against a lifetime chargeable transfer, it can be carried forward for one year and aggregated with the following year's annual exemption. Chargeable gifts made in the following year will first be set against that year's exemption and then against the unrelieved balance brought forward from the previous year. Any exemption which is carried forward but not utilised in the following year will be lost.

An individual transfers £1,000 to a discretionary trust in year 1 and £4,000 to the trust in year 2.

		£
Year 1	Chargeable transfer	1,000
	Less Annual exemption	(3,000)
	Exemption carried forward	(2,000)
Year 2	Chargeable transfer	4,000
	Less Annual exemption for the year	(3,000)
	Annual exemption brought forward	(2,000)
	Loss of annual exemption from year 1	£1,000

As lifetime gifts between individuals are potentially exempt this annual exemption is likely to become less important. Although it is not available on death it can reduce a lifetime gift which becomes chargeable because the donor dies within seven years.

An individual gifts £20,000 to his son and dies within seven years. He made no gifts in the previous year.

	£
Chargeable gift	20,000
Less Annual exemption (year of gift and previous year)	(6,000)
Chargeable gift (subject to tapering relief)	£14,000

The small gifts exemption

This applies to outright gifts of £250 or less to an individual but cannot apply if the total made to that individual exceeds £250 for that tax year. There is no limit to the number of small gifts which can be covered by this exemption. For example a person could gift, say, £200 to eight individuals, the total gifts of £1,600 would be exempt and the £3,000 annual exemption would not be reduced.

Normal expenditure exemption

Gifts can be exempt if they are claimed as part of the donor's normal expenditure. To qualify the gifts must be covered by the donor's income after deducting tax and other annual living expenses. An example of a gift which forms part of normal annual expenditure is the premium on a life policy.

> An individual has income of £50,000, expenditure of £25,000, pays tax of £15,000 and life assurance premiums of £5,000 each year for the benefit of his children.
>
> | | £ | £ |
> |---|---|---|
> | Income | | 50,000 |
> | Expenditure | (25,000) | |
> | Tax | (15,000) | |
> | | | (40,000) |
> | Net excess before gift | | 10,000 |
> | Gift — life assurance premium | | (5,000) |
> | Net excess after gift | | £5,000 |

Gifts in consideration of marriage

The exemption limits are:

—£5,000 from each parent
—£2,500 from each grandparent
—£1,000 from any other person

Certain other exempt gifts

1) To charity (during lifetime or at death) without limit;
2) A gift to a qualifying political party;
3) A gift for national purpose (such as a gift to The National Gallery or The British Museum);
4) A gift for public benefit (such as a gift of an historic building to a non-profit making trust);
5) A gift of heritage property and works of art etc, which remains in private ownership if the public is given reasonable access to it and it is kept in good order;
6) Maintenance funds for historical buildings etc;

7) Certain gifts for the support and maintenance of children and dependent relatives;

8) A disposition not intended to confer gratuitous benefit (this should cover freely negotiated transactions which were made broadly at a commercial price and transfers of property under a Divorce Court Order).

Certain of the above gifts may be exempt so long as various conditions are met with regard to the property.

Gifting to charity

You may wish to gift part of your wealth to charity. You could gift income, in which case income tax savings can be made, or capital giving an opportunity for capital gains tax and IHT savings. The gift could be made to your own charitable trust or company or directly to the charity concerned. Payments to charity could include your annual church or synagogue subscription.

Gifting income by way of deed of covenant can be an extremely tax-efficient way of passing on your wealth to charity (or to your charitable trust). The covenant will require that an amount is paid each year for more than three years ('four years'). If you wish to make a once only payment then it can be paid by loan covenant so that the gift is deemed to be made over four years and tax relief will be received over the four year period. It is possible to write the covenant in such a way that certain income is effectively paid over to charity, for example the dividends you receive from your company each year for the next four years. The income tax benefits to both the donor and the charity can be substantial as the following example shows.

An individual receives remuneration and investment income of £70,000 including net dividends from his company of £7,500 which he wishes to donate to charity.

	Net Cost £
Donor	
Net dividends covenanted to charity	7,500
Less Income tax relief	(1,500)
Net Cost	**6,000**
Charity	
Net donation under deed of covenant	7,500
Add Basic rate tax repayment	2,500
Total receipt	10,000

If during your lifetime you wish to gift large sums which exceed your income or you wish to bequeath part of your estate to charity then the deed of covenant route may not be appropriate, as you will be gifting capital rather than income. As gifts to charity are exempt for IHT purposes the net cost of a bequest to charity may be greatly reduced by the IHT relief.

	£	£
An individual has wealth of £500,000.		
If estate left to son — gross estate	500,000	
— IHT	(156,000)	
		344,000
If £100,000 left to charity, balance to son		
— to son	500,000	
— to charity	(100,000)	
	400,000	
— IHT	(116,000)	
		284,000
Net cost of gift to charity		£60,000

Business property relief

This relief is given by reducing the value transferred as set out below:

Asset transferred	Relief
	%
—A business or interest in a business	50
—Shares in a trading company giving more than 25% control by the donor and his spouse*	50
—Shares in a trading company giving not more than 25% control by the donor and his spouse*	30
—Land, buildings, machinery or plant used by a business carried on by the donor's partnership or company	30
* The non qualifying activities of a company are explained in Appendix 10.	

For the purpose of this relief 'business' includes Lloyd's Underwriting and owning commercial woodlands. The relief will also apply to Stock Exchange market makers and discount houses as from 'Big Bang'. Non-business assets owned by a business or company will reduce the available relief. The business property must be owned by the donor throughout the two years before the gift (or replace property which was owned during two of the last five years).

If the gift of business property is chargeable because it was made within seven years of the death of the donor it must be held by the donee up to the donor's death and still be business property at that time for relief to be given. It is possible for the assets gifted to be replaced by other business property without giving rise to a withdrawal of relief.

Agricultural property relief

A definition of agricultural property is set out in Appendix 10. The relief can also apply to shares in a company owning agricultural property which is controlled by the donor and his spouse. The relief is 30% of the value transferred unless one of the following applies, in which case the relief may be increased to 50%

1) the interest of the donor carried the right to vacant possession (or the right to obtain it within the next twelve months); or

2) the property has been owned by the donor since 10 March 1981 and the conditions in Appendix 10 apply.

At the date of transfer the property must have been occupied by the donor throughout the previous two years or owned throughout the period of seven years and occupied for the purposes of agriculture.

If the gift of agricultural property becomes chargeable because it was made within seven years of the death of the donor it must be held by the donee throughout the period up to the donor's death and still remain agricultural property and be occupied for the purpose of agriculture during that period, for relief to be given. It is possible for the assets gifted to be replaced by other agricultural property without giving rise to a withdrawal of relief.

Partly exempt transfers

Special provisions have been introduced to deal with partly exempt transfers. They normally operate when assets attracting business or agricultural property relief are divided among the family by virtue of a person's will. The value of specific gifts attracting relief will be their value as reduced by the relief. The provisions can best be explained by the following example.

An individual leaves a house worth £150,000 and investments of £50,000 to his wife. His will states that one-half of the shares in his family company are to be left to his wife and one-half to his children. The shares are worth £800,000 and qualify for 50% business property relief.

	£000	£000
Value of gifts to widow		
House		150
Investments		50
Business property £800,000 × 50%	400	
Less Relief	(200)	
		200
		400
Value of gifts to children		
Business property £800,000 × 50%	400	
Less Relief	(200)	
		200

The ways of giving

Generally

Once you have decided to gift assets to your dependants so as to mitigate the impact of IHT, it is then necessary to consider how the assets are to be transferred. Clearly the simplest method is to gift the asset outright to, say, your children. This would involve the passing of cash or the registering of an asset in the name of your children.

Gifting income

A popular way for taxpayers to gift to beneficiaries who had little income used to be by way of deed of covenant. However, the tax advantages of this method of giving to individuals were taken away in the Chancellor's 1988 Budget. Covenants are now only tax-effective when made out in favour of charities.

Generation skipping

It is important to consider not only the IHT position of the donor but also the donee's circumstances. If the prospective donee is wealthy or is likely to become wealthy then the asset gifted may escape IHT on the donor's death only to be taxed on the death of the donee (if the asset is in his estate or has been gifted on or within seven years of death).

In these circumstances it may be better to gift, for example, directly to your grand-children rather than to your son so that no charge will arise on your son's death.

Trusts in general

Although gifting outright is the most straightforward and, in some cases, the most tax-efficient way of estate planning it is not always the most practical method. The main problem arises from the fact that you have lost control over the asset which has been gifted. If that asset is shares in your family company the voting powers attaching to those shares will no longer be under your control and this can be a problem if the new owner of the shares should decide to vote against you.

You may wish to provide for your family but feel that they may not invest your gift wisely. If the gift is to minor children they may not be capable of looking after their wealth.

These problems can be overcome by transferring the assets into a trust. Because the trust can be drawn up in accordance with your wishes (which may be very different from individual to individual) various forms of trust have emerged and these are summarised below.

The bare trust

Assets transferred to a bare trust are held by the trustees for a named beneficiary (or beneficiaries) who has an absolute and unconditional title to both the capital and income. It is really an outright gift with the trustee holding the assets in name only and, once over 18 years old, the beneficiary can insist that the assets are transferred into his name at any time. Because of this, even if the settlor is also a trustee he has little control over the assets gifted.

The bare trust is often used when a parent gifts to a minor child. The asset will be held on bare trust so that the parent can exercise control over it until the child reaches the age of 18 or marries. The tax treatment in respect of the income which accrues from the asset gifted can be more favourable than if an outright gift had been made. In the case of an outright gift the income is taxed on the parent until the child reaches the age of 18. It is understood that, if the income from an asset held on bare trust is accumulated and not paid to the child during his or her unmarried infancy, it is treated as the child's income. (Care needs to be exercised to ensure that the transaction does not fall within the anti-avoidance provisions relating to settlements and also loan arrangements.) This benefit is illustrated below.

An individual is a 40% tax payer. He wishes to gift £50,000 to his 15 year old son and invest the money on the money market at say 12% gross per annum.		
Income tax position on absolute gift	£	£
Gross interest £50,000 × 12%	6,000	
Less Income tax 40%	(2,400)	
Net return		3,600
Potential income tax position on bare trust		
Gross interest as above	6,000	
Less Income tax (£6,000−£2,605 = £3,395 × 25%)	(849)	
Net return		5,151
Benefit		£1,551

Accumulation and maintenance trust — 'A & M trust'

Although the bare trust may provide the parent with some control over the assets gifted, this only applies until the child reaches 18 years of age, when absolute control passes to the child. Many parents may wish to protect their gift by retaining control indefinitely.

One solution to this problem may well be the A & M trust which can be drawn up in an extremely flexible manner. In addition, it is also very tax-efficient and does not attract an IHT charge when it is formed irrespective of the value of the gift. This is because a lifetime gift to an A & M trust is treated in the same way as a direct gift to an individual. The amount gifted is exempt so long as the settlor survives for seven years and there is no IHT charge when the trust assets are distributed to the beneficiaries.

This favourable treatment will apply so long as the following conditions are met:

1) one or more beneficiaries will by the age of 25 become entitled to at least an interest in the income of the trust; and

2) no interest in possession exists at present and the income of the trust is to be accumulated or applied for the maintenance, education or benefit of a beneficiary. This could enable income to be applied for school fees, clothing etc.

The A & M trust is suitable for children or grandchildren as the beneficiaries must be either:

1) grandchildren of a common grandparent, or

2) children, widows or widowers of such grandchildren who were themselves beneficiaries but who died before the time when, had they survived, they would have become entitled to benefit.

Illegitimate, adopted and stepchildren can be included as beneficiaries. As you will see from the above comments it is possible to draw up an A & M trust deed so that the beneficiaries (who may include as yet unborn children) only receive an interest in the income at age 25 but do not become entitled to the capital of the trust until, say, age 40 or earlier at the discretion of the trustees. As the settlor can also be a trustee he will be able to gift while retaining effective control over the assets for a considerable period of time. This may be particularly important if he wishes to gift shares in the family company. As trustee he would be able to decide how much and when income is paid to each beneficiary. If the only asset of the trust is shares in the company which does not pay any dividends to its shareholders, then the beneficiaries would receive no income and might have to wait a considerable period of time before they receive anything from the trust.

Any income which is accumulated within the trust will be subject to income tax at an effective rate of 35%. However the tax charge can be effectively reduced by paying income to the beneficiaries who will then be able to reclaim tax if their marginal income tax rate is less than 35%. The payment may need to be deferred until the beneficiary is 18 if the settlor is his or her parent so as to avoid adverse income tax implications.

Interest in possession trust

While the A & M trust is probably the most tax-efficient and flexible form of trust, as the beneficiary must become entitled to at least an interest in the income by the age of 25 it cannot be used when gifting to individuals who are already over 25. In such cases the interest in possession trust may be the next best vehicle.

Under the interest in possession trust the beneficiaries (usually called life tenants) must from the outset have a right to the income of the trust or the use of the property within the trust. Again the trustees will be able to control the investment of the trust's assets, and gifts into (or out of) the trust will escape IHT so long as the donor (or life tenant) survives the gift by seven years.

The value of the asset in which the interest subsists is deemed to belong to the beneficiary. Therefore that asset will be taxed as part of his estate unless the interest is gifted on more than seven years before his death. The gifting of a life interest is a potentially exempt transfer based upon the value of the underlying asset of the trust fund. If the donor survives for seven years then no IHT charge will arise.

Interest in possession trusts are useful if a person wishes to plan the method in which his wealth is to be distributed while ensuring that the capital is not squandered. For example, if he and his wife have children from previous marriages he may wish to protect his wife during her lifetime but ensure that his wealth passes to his, rather than her, children on her death. For this reason he may not wish to gift outright to his wife but settle funds in trust for himself during his lifetime, his wife during her lifetime and his children after her death.

Discretionary trust

This is the most flexible of all the trusts but the least attractive for IHT purposes. It enables the settlor to leave his options open by gifting wealth into a trust and naming the individuals who can benefit but leave the trustees (who could include the settlor) with full discretion as to who receives income or capital and when such payments are to be made. If the settlor is one of the beneficiaries the gifts with reservation rules will apply. Although a person may be included in the class of beneficiaries he or she may never receive any benefit from the trust.

The discretionary trust is given special treatment for IHT purposes. Tax charges may arise on the following events:

1) Creation of the trust: a lifetime gift to a discretionary trust.

2) On each tenth anniversary of the trust.

3) On a capital distribution from the trust.

The ten yearly charge is calculated at 30% of the IHT rates which apply to lifetime transfers so that the maximum charge is 6% of the value of the fund every ten years.

It is possible to avoid these charges. If the gift into trust is not taxed because it falls within the nil rate band of £110,000 and the trust is broken before the tenth anniversary, no charge would arise on the capital distributed. Therefore an asset worth, say, £110,000 could be settled and distributed nine years later when it was worth, say, £500,000 without an IHT charge arising.

Under the present rules a discretionary trust can enable a donor to gift into trust and have a breathing space of just under ten years before deciding who will benefit from the fund. A husband and wife could each gift £110,000 into their discretionary trust so that a total of £220,000 could be gifted without incurring IHT. However, if the donor died within seven years of his gift, the IHT on his estate at death would be adversely affected.

If the settlor wishes to have the option of becoming a beneficiary under the trust at some future time, the trust deed could allow for the class of beneficiaries to be extended at the discretion of the trustees. However, if this option is exercised, the gifts with reservation rules are likely to apply. Although this arrangement may have adverse income tax implications, this may not be a problem if little income is received by the trust, possibly because shares in the family company have been settled. In view of the tax implications arising from this form of settlement, professional advice should always be sought before proceeding.

Trusts — IHT and income tax

The table below shows when an IHT charge arises in respect of the various trusts and indicates the income tax position (assuming the settlor or his wife are not beneficiaries).

	Form of trust			
	Bare	Interest in possession	A & M	Discretionary
IHT				
Gift into trust more than seven years before death	No	No	No	Yes
Capital distribution out of trust to beneficiary	No	No	No	Yes
Retention of asset in trust for ten years	No	No	No	Yes
Income Tax	Income assessed on beneficiary		Trustees pay 35%	

Asset selection

Generally

Having established that you wish to pass wealth to your dependants it is then necessary to re-examine your capital statement and net spendable income schedules. If you refer to the example in Appendices 2 to 7, you will see that as net income exceeds expenditure, it may be possible to gift income-producing assets without jeopardising the donor's financial position. The following example illustrates this.

Gift of, say, £30,000 from building society accounts.	
	£
Loss of gross income £30,000 at say, 10%	3,000
Tax thereon £3,000 × 40%	(1,200)
Loss of net income	1,800
Surplus income as per Appendix 5	3,733
Revised surplus income	£1,933

Non-income producing assets

Before gifting assets which will lead to a reduction in net spendable income, it is advisable to consider what other assets could be gifted. The capital statement in Appendix 2 shows that the following assets are not income-producing (after deducting any interest payable) so that if they were to be gifted, no loss of income would arise.

Asset	Value
	£000
The home (less mortgage)	190
Investment property (less loans)	40
Shares in the family trading company	360

Practical difficulties may arise from a gift of the home (or contents of the home) and in addition the gifts with reservation rules would normally apply.

The investment property (together with its related loans) could be gifted. It does not produce any net income as the rental income is matched by the interest payable on the loan to acquire the property.

The shares in the family trading company are not income-producing if the company has not paid any dividends. However, remuneration is drawn from the company and if, in future, dividends rather than remuneration are to be paid, possibly to avoid national insurance, there could be a loss of future income if the shares were gifted. The life policies are also not income-producing and could be gifted.

Appreciating assets

Whilst rapidly appreciating assets are good investments, they aggravate the IHT problem. For this reason, it is advisable to gift such assets as early as possible.

One such example could be the investment property mentioned above. The property may be worth more unencumbered than if it has a sitting tenant. By gifting a property when it has a sitting tenant it may be possible to agree a relatively low value with the Inland Revenue authorities so that if the gift is chargeable, less tax will be payable.

Shares in new ventures can be rapidly appreciating assets but estate planning is often overlooked when the venture is set up. It may be advisable to ensure that some shares are held for your dependants from the outset. There should be no IHT to pay as the shares in the new venture should have little value until the trade has been established. A parallel company could be set up as a subsidiary or associate of the main trading company with some shares being owned by your dependants. New ventures can be passed through such a company, but if existing business is transferred there could be a transfer of goodwill which could lead to both a capital gains tax and an IHT charge.

The family home

The family home is the asset which is least likely to be gifted because of the emotional and financial security which attaches to it. In addition such a gift is likely to be caught by the gifts with reservation rules as may the household contents and chattels. To ensure that these rules are avoided, a full market rent may need to be paid if the home is to be gifted to the dependants, with a tenancy arrangement which will allow the donor to continue to live there. The cost to both donor and donee can be substantial but as explained in the chapter on gifts with reservation another possibility is the carve-out method.

The treatment of gifting a share of a house was dealt with by Mr Brooke for the Government in the Parliamentary Standing Committee debates who said, '... it may be that my Hon. Friend's intention concerns the common case where someone gives away an individual share in land, typically a house, which is then occupied by all the joint owners including the donor. For example, elderly parents make unconditional gifts of undivided shares in their house to their children and the parents and the children occupy the property as their family home, each owner bearing his or her share of the running costs. In those circumstances, the parents' occupation or enjoyment of the part of the house that they have given away is in return for similar enjoyment of the children of the other part of the property. Thus the donor's occupation is for a full consideration ... the gifts with reservation rules will not be applied ...'

Although major problems may arise from a gift of the family home, it may be much easier for tax purposes to gift a second home, such as a holiday home. This asset will often be non-income producing and so long as the donor can occupy it when he wishes he may be happy to gift it. If, for example, he owns a villa in Spain which he uses one month a year and the rest of the time it is left vacant, he may be willing to gift it, pay a market rent for its use and so avoid the gifts with reservation rules. The donee can use the rent to meet certain of the expenses of the villa, but the donor may also need to settle cash to enable the donee to meet all the expenses.

Gift of villa in Spain worth, say, £100,000 to A & M trust for children. Market rent for its use for one month a year, say, £750. Donor dies ten years later when the villa is worth £200,000 and his estate is £500,000. The UK tax implications would be as follows:		
	£	£
Donor		
Annual payment of		(750)
A & M Trust		
Rental income	750	
Expenses of letting period, say	(150)	
	600	
Tax	(210)	
	390	
Expenses for non-letting period, say	(3,000)	
Excess to be met from, say, further cash injection		(2,610)
Estate		
Value of villa on death	200,000	
IHT saving at 40%		80,000

Interest-free loans

In addition to a gift of wealth the estate planner may wish to consider lending funds to his dependants so that they may enjoy the income from the loan or the future appreciation of assets acquired. In this way the lender has 'frozen' his assets. However, there are anti-avoidance provisions which need to be considered in this regard.

In order to show that no IHT charge arises, the interest-free loan arrangement must be formalised by a written document showing that it is repayable on demand. The interest-free loan could be repaid over a number of years in amounts equal to the loss of net income by the lender so that he is in no worse a position financially. Of course, the lender will need to be confident that the borrower can or will repay the loan and so may need to receive some form of security. If part of the loan is outstanding at the lender's death it will form part of his estate.

The family trading company

Generally

The make up of an estate varies from person to person but a large part of the estate of a wealthy businessman will often comprise the value of shares in his family trading company. The company may be very profitable and enable its owner to maintain a very high standard of living. Remuneration (and pension contributions) or dividends from the company together with personal expenses met by the company (e.g. such as the provision and maintenance of a car together with the payment of all private petrol) may more than cover his annual living expenditure and ensure that his financial position is secure. Its continued success may also provide security for future generations.

Meeting the tax liability

The incidence of IHT on the shares in the family trading company can cause a severe problem if no planning is carried out.

An estate of £1.6m comprises a house worth £200,000, investments of £100,000 and shares in the family trading company worth £1.3m.

	£000
Value of estate	1,600
Business property relief, say, £1.3m × 50%	(650)
Chargeable estate	950
IHT	336
Sale of assets to pay the tax	
— House	200
— Investments	100
	300
Shortfall	36

Although the tax in respect of the house and shares can be paid by instalments over ten years the shortfall will need to be met by extracting funds from the company, increasing the funds available from the investments held and the sale of the house so as to increase the £300,000 which is available to £336,000. This example would paint a more dramatic picture if no business property relief were to be available on death (possibly because the company was or had become an investment or land dealing company). In that case approximately £600,000 would be payable on death, a shortfall of £300,000. If only 30% business property relief is available (if for example the deceased owned less than 25% of the company) then the tax would be approximately £440,000, a shortfall of £140,000.

This impact of IHT on death not only arises where the estate owns shares in a private company. For example, a family may have sufficient shares in a public company to block a potential take-over bid and the need to sell shares to pay the tax on death could seriously affect the family's position.

Valuation

Normally it is easy to determine the value of the gift for IHT purposes but in the case of shares in an unquoted family company, a share valuation will be necessary. The transfer will reflect the amount by which the value of the donor's estate has been reduced. It will be necessary to consider the value of the shareholding both before and after the gift and a discount will need to be applied to holdings of less than 100% of the issued share capital of the company. For example, a 10% shareholding is worth less than 10% of the value of the company as its voting rights have little influence over the affairs of the company. The effect of the discounts which are applied to a gift of shares in a private company can produce surprising results.

An individual owns all the issued share capital in a company which is valued at £1m and wishes to gift a 30% interest to a discretionary trust. If the agreed discounts which are applicable to the following shareholding interests are as shown below the chargeable transfer will be as follows:

Shareholding	Discount
%	%
100	0
30	50
70	20

Chargeable transfer

	£
Value of holding before gift £1m × 100%	1,000,000
Value of holding after gift £1m × 70% less 20% discount	560,000
Transfer for IHT purposes	£440,000
Value of asset held by discretionary trust £1m × 30% less 50% discount	£150,000

Gifting shares in the family company

Shares in the family trading company may be the ideal asset to gift. If no dividends are paid by the company because the shareholders draw profits as remuneration, then a gift of shares will not affect the donor's net spendable income. (However it should be borne in mind that dividends may be paid in future so as to avoid employer's national insurance, which is currently chargeable on remuneration but not dividends.) If the company is successful its shares may be the most sharply appreciating asset in the estate and any future appreciation will only aggravate the IHT position.

If the shares are to be gifted to, say an interest in possession trust, their value will need to be carefully considered to determine whether an IHT charge will arise. If the company is likely to become more profitable in the next few years then the gift may need to be made as soon as possible as the value of the shares will be increasing. If you wish to avoid an immediate IHT charge, an estate freezing exercise may need to be considered, possibly by having a bonus issue of preference or deferred ordinary shares so that the future growth accrues free of IHT.

A problem which may be encountered is the possibility that the donor may wish to ensure that he does not jeopardise his control over major policy decisions affecting the company. Appendix 13 illustrates the importance of various levels of shareholding interest. If, for example, the shares of the company are held equally by the donor and his brother, and he gifts one share to say his son then voting control could shift to his brother if his son were to side with his brother on an issue affecting the company.

The problem could be overcome by gifting into trust. If the gift is to an interest in possession trust or an accumulation and maintenance trust, there will be no adverse IHT implications. In this way the donor may be able to pass wealth to his dependants while effectively retaining control over the voting rights of the shares. The gift could ensure that shares in the family company do not need to be sold to pay the tax on death.

Facts as per the example at the beginning of this chapter except the deceased gifted some shares in the family company eight years before his death.	
Estate on death	*£000*
House	200
Investments	100
Shares in family trading company	800
	1100
Less Business property relief at, say, 50%	(400)
	700
IHT (covered by value of house and investments)	236

As you will see from the above, business property relief can be very valuable. In the past there was a benefit in reducing a personal holding to below 25% as the value of a small minority interest can be heavily discounted. However as business property relief can now fall from 50% to 30% on the retained shareholding if that holding falls to 25%, it may now be advisable to gift so that the retained shareholding is less than 50% of the equity share capital but more than a 25% interest.

In the past it was important to equalise interest between the husband and wife to utilise the lower rate bands. However now that there is only a nil rate and a 40% band this process is much easier. It is merely necessary to ensure that each spouse has net chargeable assets of £110,000 which can be left to, say, the children.

Another way of protecting against the IHT charge on shares in the family company (or any other assets) is to gift shares to a charitable trust which can be formed by the family. The settlor could be a trustee and so effectively control the voting rights of the shares. Any dividends paid by the company may be received tax-free by the charity and a tax repayment claim could be made in respect of the tax credit which arises from the dividend.

By using the charitable trust the value of the shares is taken outside the family as the shares must be held for charitable purposes, but voting control of the company can be retained within the family. It may be used if the donor no longer wishes to gift any further assets during his lifetime and the family wants to ensure that measures are taken now so that the shares need not be sold on death. The shares would be gifted to the charitable trust during lifetime or on death by amending the will.

Facts as per the example at the beginning of the chapter. Shares in the family trading company worth £180,000 are bequeathed to the family charitable trust on death.

Chargeable estate	£000
Shares in family trading company	1300
Less Bequest of shares to charitable trust	(180)
Value of remaining shares, say	1120
Less Business property relief at, say, 50%	(560)
	560
House	200
Investments	100
	860
IHT thereon	300
Tax paid by sale of house and investments	300

The business and agricultural property relief trap

As shown above, substantial tax savings can be achieved if the assets attract business or agricultural property relief. However, these reliefs can be wasted if they are not available when the tax charge arises.

Often married couples will leave most of their wealth to each other so that the bulk of the tax arises on the death of the surviving spouse; inter-spouse gifts during lifetime and on death are normally exempt from charge. Therefore the critical time when the relief can be of benefit is on the second death.

It is often the case that the wife survives her husband. If his trading company is the estate's principal asset, the wife may wish to sell the company after his death, especially as her husband may have been the driving force behind it. If she sells the company she will receive cash which can be reinvested to produce the income which is required to replace her husband's remuneration from the company. The problem is that she will now have replaced an asset which attracted relief with cash which gives rise to no relief, so that more tax will be payable on her death. Business property relief can also be lost if the asset is not held for two years before it is given away.

In these circumstances, it may be advisable for the husband, on his death to leave shares in the company, rather than other non-business assets, to his children so that the relief applies.

Tax-efficient investments

Generally

Having determined the value of an estate and the potential IHT, it is worth reviewing the assets comprising the estate. An individual may not wish to gift any assets during his lifetime, but could be interested in changing the mix of his estate.

By acquiring assets which give rise to IHT relief and disposing of assets which do not, the value of the estate may not change but the IHT charge may fall. In addition, the tax may be payable by instalments over a ten-year period rather than in full six months after the death of the donor. Of course, the capital gains tax position will need to be examined to ensure that a charge does not arise, and the commercial implications of such action must be examined at the outset, to ensure that the assets to be acquired will appreciate as fast and provide as much net income after tax as before. The assets which attract relief are set out in the section dealing with exemptions and reliefs.

The benefit from reinvesting money in business property can be seen from the following:

Assets	Estate not attracting relief	Estate attracting relief at 50%
	£000	£000
Business property	—	400
House and contents etc	200	200
Investments and bank deposits	700	300
	900	900
IHT	316	236
Potential tax saving		80

Shares in a private trading company

Business property relief is available in respect of trades and business assets. As explained above, even if a shareholder does not control a private trading company, 50% business property relief may be available. It is possible to acquire shares which attract business expansion scheme relief, provide an exemption from capital gains tax and also produce business property relief for IHT purposes. The cost of these shares to a taxpayer with a large estate could be significantly reduced by these reliefs.

An individual with an estate of £500,000 receives income of £60,000 p.a. He acquires shares in a private trading company and will leave his estate to his son.

	£	£
Cost of shares		10,000
Income tax relief £10,000 at 40%	4,000	
Potential IHT savings £10,000 at,		
say, 30% × 40%	1,200	
		(5,200)
Net cost after tax reliefs		£4,800

Woodlands

The acquisition of a woodlands estate is a long-term investment (normally a minimum of ten years) which can provide capital gains tax and IHT savings and also qualify for government grants. Woodlands can be acquired at various stages of development and certain trees can take fifty years to reach their full size. In the past, it was possible to obtain income tax relief for expenditure incurred on planting trees, maintaining the estate and paying interest on a loan to finance the investment. Also, any timber sales were effectively tax-free. The work involved would normally be undertaken by professional forestry managers rather than the investor himself. The relief was abolished in the Finance Act 1988 so that such expenditure no longer produces an income tax shelter but any income from woodlands is free of income tax. There is transitional continuing relief until 5 April 1993 for those who were obtaining income tax relief before 15 March 1988. To offset the withdrawal of relief, a system of grants for planting trees has been extended. When the estate is sold, the value of the trees escapes capital gains tax.

For IHT purposes, 50% of the value of the standing timber may attract relief so that only one half of the asset is chargeable. Any tax may then be paid in ten equal annual instalments so that there is a significant tax deferral as well as a tax saving. It is also possible to elect within two years of death that no tax is payable on that death. Instead the value of the standing timber is taxed as the top slice of the deceased's estate when the trees are sold, but the charge arises on the proceeds received rather than the value at death. In this way a further tax deferral can be achieved as the woodlands could be held for say a further twenty years before the tax is payable on its sale, although any increase in value since death will be caught.

The increase in the value of woodlands has generally beaten inflation in recent years but the appreciation has not been dramatic. The grants can be generous so that the net cost is significantly reduced. A woodlands investment is worth considering if the investor wishes to pass wealth to his dependants on death in a tax-efficient manner. However the effect that the withdrawal of income tax relief for investors will have on forestry prices in the next few years will need to be borne in mind.

Agricultural property

As explained earlier, agricultural property can also give rise to relief of up to 50% of the value transferred. Also the tax on agricultural property which is part of an estate can be paid in ten equal annual instalments.

As with any investment, it is important to consider whether it is the right time to buy agricultural property. The commercial implications of such action should always take precedence over the taxation ramifications.

Becoming a Lloyd's underwriter

Anyone who can show wealth of over £100,000 in readily realisable assets (£250,000 from early 1990) and can pass the Lloyd's means test can become a Lloyd's underwriter. By doing so, you can effectively make your his wealth work twice for you as an underwriter is required to deposit assets with Lloyd's so that they can be used as security for his underwriting activities but he continues to derive income and capital gains from these funds. He will then share in the underwriting profits or losses of his syndicate. As premiums are received by syndicates in advance of any claims they also produce income and tax-free capital gains from the investment of the money, part of which is normally in gilts.

An underwriter can lose as well as make money from Lloyd's. His liability is unlimited but his level of risk can be reduced by 'stop loss' insurance. In recent years losses have been made by a number of syndicates within Lloyd's, so syndicate selection is vitally important.

Although this activity should be approached with caution it can be both profitable and produce IHT savings. This is because it is treated as a trade and so 50% business property relief can be obtained on some if not all of the Lloyd's funds.

Gifting on death

Making a will

In most cases a will is important to ensure that your assets are distributed to your family according to your wishes and in a tax-efficient manner. Its existence may also speed up the administrative procedures so that the beneficiaries can obtain the assets earlier. In addition, you can ensure that the estate is handled by responsible executors and that guardians are appointed to look after your children. Although the making of a will may involve some time and professional costs these need not be large and it is surprising how many people die without making a will. Once made, a will should be regularly reviewed to take account of your changing financial position and family circumstances, in particular in the event of marriage, divorce or the birth of children.

If no will is made the intestacy rules will apply. These are set out in Appendix 11 and you will see that they could result in your estate being distributed in a completely different manner from the way in which you would want to leave your wealth.

An individual has assets of £500,000 excluding any personal possessions and wishes to leave £70,000 to his children with the balance to his wife. This distribution of his estate would avoid any IHT charge on death. However, under the rules of intestacy the estate would be distributed as follows:

	£
Assets to wife — absolutely	75,000
— held in trust	212,500
Assets held in trust for children	212,500
	500,000
Inheritance tax payable	(41,000)
	£459,000

Using the nil rate band

The nil rate band of £110,000 is applicable to individuals. Husband and wife have separate bands. Often married couples arrange for all their assets to be left to each other so that a charge only arises on the second death. This can be inefficient for tax purposes (although it may be necessary for other reasons) as it means that no use will be made of the nil rate band on the first death. Substantial savings can be made by revising the wills so that certain assets are passed to other beneficiaries on death.

An individual has an estate of £400,000. He leaves a wife and two children. The estate is worth £500,000 on his wife's death.

	Tax on second death
	£
All assets left to spouse	156,000
All assets apart from £110,000 left to spouse	112,000
Saving	£44,000

In the past, it was important to equalise estates to ensure that both spouses had sufficient wealth to take advantage of the lower rates of IHT. Now this technique is only relevant in so far as ensuring that they both have wealth of £110,000 so as to utilise the nil rate band.

As many estates do not exceed £250,000, the above technique can be one of the most important. It may be possible to use the nil rate band on the first death by gifting an interest in the home to the children. If the house is owned by both spouses it will be necessary to ensure that it is held as tenants in common and not under a joint tenancy arrangement. Consideration will need to be given as to the surviving spouse's rights so that he or she cannot be evicted in the future if, say, a family rift occurs while the children own a part of the home. The children's interest could be left by way of a will trust but clearly professional advice should be sought before the will is drafted.

Gifting after death

At the time when you draw up your will you may not know what your financial and tax position (and that of your spouse and your family) is likely to be at the time of your death.

A solution to this problem could be to write your will on a discretionary basis. The will sets out the distribution of assets in the way in which you currently wish to dispose of them, but it gives the executors discretionary powers to override those provisions and re-distribute the assets among the beneficiaries named or identified in the will. The surviving spouse can be named as one of the personal representatives so as to have absolute control over the way in which the estate is distributed.

This form of will may be suitable if maximum flexibility is required from the outset. Provided the assets are distributed within two years of death, the distribution is treated as having been made by the deceased at the time of his death and no adverse tax consequences should arise. This flexibility may enable the spouse and beneficiaries to distribute the estate in the most tax-efficient way, possibly by utilising the nil rate band, making maximum use of the reliefs attaching to certain assets, generation skipping etc.

Tax planning measures can be used by the beneficiaries even if the deceased's will was not written on a discretionary basis. This is because the beneficiaries have two years from the date of death to review the family's financial and taxation position. If they agree that the assets of the estate could be distributed in a more efficient manner, a deed of variation can be drawn up so that the will is effectively revised (or if no will was drawn up, the transfers according to the rules of intestacy may be revised). Such action will require the consent of the beneficiary who will be giving up wealth and an election must be submitted to the Inland Revenue within six months of making the deed of variation.

A problem can arise, however, if the will leaves assets in trust for minor children. This is because if those assets are to be re-directed it will generally require consent of the Court. This can be a costly and time-consuming exercise. Normally the assets will have been left in trust for the children due to the deceased's wishes. However, in some cases the will as originally drafted may have been very tax-efficient at the time but should have been revised as the tax legislation changed.

There should be no adverse inheritance or capital gains tax implications in making the deed of variation but if one of the beneficiaries is directing certain of the assets to his minor children, the income from those assets could be taxable on him until the children reach the age of 18. Substantial IHT savings can be made by effectively revising the terms of the will, for example, if the nil rate band has not been utilised. A deed of variation may be particularly suitable if the deceased has left surplus assets to the spouse, who feels that certain wealth could be immediately passed on to the family so as to mitigate the eventual IHT charge on her death.

Husband and wife

Generally

Transferring assets between spouses has always been one of the more popular ways of estate planning. Legal ownership can be passed on with no capital gains tax penalty whilst the donor (within a stable marriage) will usually still have access to any income from the asset. Such transfers are normally exempt from IHT. However, if one of the parties to a marriage is not domiciled in the UK then only £55,000 may be gifted by the UK domiciled spouse without receiving an IHT charge under present legislation.

Using the nil rate band

As explained earlier, savings can be made by using the nil rate band on the first death, to gift assets to a beneficiary other than the surviving spouse. This can obviously only happen if the deceased had assets to give away, so it may be necessary to transfer assets between husband and wife during their lifetime.

Tax savings can be maximised by fully utilising the nil rate band on the first death or by ensuring that each spouse has assets of £110,000 to give away. Assets of £110,000 each could be gifted into, say, a discretionary trust without an IHT charge arising on the initial transfer.

	£	£
Assets held by the husband	1,000,000	
Assets held by the wife	Nil	
Total estate	1,000,000	
Will drafted so that estate goes to wife		
Tax on first death	Nil	
Tax on second death		356,000
Tax payable if £110,000 transferred during lifetime to wife who passes this wealth to the children on death		
Tax on first death	Nil	
Tax on second death		312,000
Saving		£44,000

Clearly it may not be possible to achieve these savings as sufficient funds will need to be left to ensure that the spouse has adequate income to meet future living expenses. Of course, an estate could be efficiently equalised during lifetime but unless the wills are correctly drawn up, the benefits can be lost if, say, all assets then revert to the spouse on death.

The family trading company

A benefit can arise by spreading shares in the family trading company between husband and wife. This is because although when valuing the shares those held by husband and wife must be aggregated, when a gift is made, it is only necessary to consider the reduction in the value of the estate of the donor and not the donor's spouse. The benefit is explained by the following example:

An individual has held 45% and his wife 10% of the shares of a private trading company. They wish to gift a 10% interest to an interest in possession trust for their children. The value of the relevant shareholding interests in the company are set out below.

55% interest	£550,000	
45% interest	£350,000	

	Chargeable transfer	
Gift by wife	*£000*	*£000*
10% shareholding valued for IHT purposes £550,000 × 10/55		100
Gift by husband (assuming he owns the entire 55% interest)		
Value of interest before gift	550	
Value of interest after gift	350	
		200
Difference in amount of chargeable transfer		100

The capital gains tax trap

As no IHT arises in respect of assets passing from the deceased to the surviving spouse, it may not therefore be advisable to give assets pregnant with gain to your spouse, especially in later years if the holder of the asset is in ill health.

In 1982, Andrew acquired 1,000 shares in a quoted company for £1,000. In 1988 he gave them to his wife, Mary, when they were worth £40,000. Andrew died in 1989 when the shares were worth £50,000 and a year later Mary sold them for £57,000.

Mary's CGT liability in 1990

Proceeds	57,500
Cost and indexation, say,	1,500
	56,000
CGT at, say, 40%	£22,400

If Andrew had not given the shares to Mary but instead had left them to her in his will, the gain up to 1989 would not be chargeable and Mary's gain in 1990 would be

Proceeds	57,000
Probate value and indexation, say	52,500
Gain	£4,500

This is covered by the annual exemption. Thus, by leaving the shares to Mary instead of giving them to her, CGT of over £20,000 could be saved.

Independent taxation

From 6 April 1990, married couples will be taxed as if they were single persons. Each spouse will be entitled to a personal allowance, separate income tax rates and a capital gains tax exemption.

Therefore there may be income and capital gains tax savings to be made by equalising estates, as well as the IHT benefits illustrated above. For example, where a husband, who pays income tax at the higher rate, has a large share portfolio and his wife has no income, he may wish to transfer part of his holdings, with the following results:

1. Her personal allowance will be wholly or partially used.

2. Income over and above the personal allowance will be taxed at 25% instead of the husband's 40% rate.

3. Her capital gains tax exemption can be set against future gains from disposing of shareholdings.

Appendix 14 illustrates the income tax benefit of independent taxation based on the information which is set out in Appendix 2.

The need for insurance

Generally

There are really two methods of dealing with the potential IHT charge. The first is to maximise lifetime gifts and to utilise the available reliefs and exemptions. However, although this planning will reduce the tax charge it is unlikely to be fully mitigated, as part of the estate may comprise the home and funds which are required to meet future living expenses. The second approach, therefore, is based upon the acceptance of an ultimate tax charge and uses life assurance as a way of providing funds for the dependants so that they can meet the tax liability. A combination of both methods will often be used in an effective estate plan.

Before examining estate planning, it is advisable to consider whether your family will be adequately protected on your death or disability.

Protecting the family

The question which needs to be asked is 'if I die tomorrow will my family be able to maintain our current standard of living?'. If the answer is no and, in particular, if the family income will be dramatically reduced, then life assurance protection will be necessary. Consider the following example.

An individual is 40 years of age and married with two young children. He is an employee earning £30,000 p.a., and his wife does not work. His assets are a house worth £100,000 (on which there is a £30,000 endowment linked mortgage) and investments of £10,000.

Net spendable income	Current position		Position after death
	£000	£000	£000
Salary		30	—
Gross income from investments (say)		1	1
		31	1
Mortgage and endowment policy payments	(3)		
Income tax	(7)		
		(10)	—
		21	1
Expenditure, say		(18)	(12)
Net surplus/(deficit)		3	(11)

The situation could be vastly improved if a life assurance policy is taken out; this would provide funds for the family in the event of death. The benefits from a policy can be inflation proof by index-linking the premium. The two main forms of life assurance are as follows:

1) Whole life assurance — various forms of whole life assurance are explained in Appendix 12;

2) Term assurance — this is suitable if you want to take out life assurance for a limited period of time.

You may believe that in ten years you will have accumulated sufficient wealth so that your family will not need to rely on life assurance so that term assurance is all that is required. There is no surrender value to these policies but they are normally cheaper because at the end of a ten-year plan you will have paid money for no return. The policy can be written to include a right to convert into a whole life policy.

Clearly the ability to take out whole life assurance will depend upon the available net spendable income and capital.

The facts as in the previous example. The individual uses his net spendable income of £3,000 and takes out a low cost whole life policy on his life. The annual premium is £1,800 and the minimum life cover £200,000.

Net spendable income position on death	£
Proceeds from policy	200,000
Other investments	10,000
	210,000
Income thereon at, say, 10% gross	21,000
Less Tax	(4,600)
	16,400
Expenditure	12,000
Surplus	£4,400

If before his death an individual was the driving force behind the family company or business, its value is likely to be materially depleted on death. Even if another director is brought in to run the company it may take some time before confidence and profitability is restored.

In these circumstances, a keyman insurance policy would be advisable so as to produce a capital sum for the company which would help to alleviate these problems. (Similar insurance cover may be required by a partnership to enable it to pay out a deceased partner's share.) The premium would normally be paid by the company and can provide corporation tax relief although any proceeds from the policy may be taxable. The tax treatment can differ depending upon the type of policy. The cost of such a policy may be comparatively modest depending upon the age of the insured. An example of the costs of a level term assurance plan to age 65 is as follows:

Man aged	Sum assured £100,000 — Annual premium
	£
30	362
40	530
50	866
60	1,095

The above rates were quoted on 25 August 1988.

Although many people cover the position should they die, they often overlook the problem which can arise if they become seriously disabled so that they cannot continue to work. This may be even more serious from the financial point of view, as not only will earnings fall or cease altogether, but there may be a request for financial assistance to provide for medical fees etc. This potential difficulty can be met by a permanent health insurance policy which will pay out regular income upon the assured becoming disabled. The policy could be taken out personally to provide for the family or by a company in respect of an employee. The scheme will normally end when the insured reaches the age of 60 or 65. The income from a policy taken out by an individual will become subject to income tax after one to two years depending upon when the benefit commences. An example of the cost involved for a policy to provide annual income of £20,000 per annum to age 65 is as follows:

Age of insured next birthday	Income cover £20,000 p.a. — Annual premium	Income cover £20,000 p.a. index linked — Annual premium
	£	£
30	250	356
40	380	458
50	640	900

The benefit commences 13 weeks after disablement.

Pensions — death in service benefits

There are various forms of non-state pensions. There is the company pension scheme for employees and directors, and the personal pension plan, the premiums from which are invested with life insurance companies, banks, building societies etc. Part of the company scheme contribution may be met by the employee, while the personal pension will often be completely funded by the individual although employers may contribute if they wish. A self-administered pension scheme may be arranged for directors or employees of a company. The pension schemes are designed to provide a pension for life, together with the option to take part of the fund as a tax-free cash sum on retirement. Death in service benefits are normally included in the scheme and this is where IHT may be mitigated.

The pension scheme will normally permit benefits which arise from death while still a director or employee of the company. On death in service, the benefit will pass to the trustees who will exercise their discretion as to who should receive the payment. The director will normally provide a letter of wishes indicating who should benefit. This is not a legally binding document but if the trustees of the scheme are, for example, his co-directors it would be unusual for them not to follow these wishes. Similar arrangements apply for personal pension plans, where life cover can be obtained and benefits can be paid directly to or in trust for the beneficiaries without an IHT charge.

The death in service benefits of a company scheme can be substantial and are normally an amount equal to four times final remuneration plus the pension benefits which the company has purchased for the beneficiaries (e.g. the wife). The maximum benefits are dependent upon the pension scheme having sufficient funds to pay out such benefits. It may be advisable for the scheme to 'top up' its funds by term assurance to ensure that the maximum benefits can be paid.

If the death in service benefits are paid to the spouse they will form part of her estate and so aggravate the IHT position. However, there is the opportunity to pay the benefits to, say, the children or grandchildren, and then they will pass directly to them without any IHT charge.

The final remuneration of an individual is £55,000. He dies in service and the pension fund has £220,000 which can be paid to his spouse (whose wealth will exceed £110,000 on her death) or his two children equally.

	£
Payment to spouse	220,000
Potential IHT at 40%	(88,000)
	132,000
Payment to children	220,000
Potential IHT on wife's death	—
	220,000
Tax saved	88,000

Providing for the tax

The impact of the IHT charge has been considered earlier and the problem which can arise if a large part of the estate comprises shares in the family business has been explained. The potential tax liability or part of that liability can be met by taking out life assurance, with the policy written for the benefit of your dependants (possibly under trust) other than your spouse, as no tax charge will arise if assets pass to your spouse on death.

The premium paid each year will be treated as a gift as the benefit of the policy will accrue to your dependants. The premiums which are made more than seven years before death will be exempt and only those made within that seven year period will be chargeable. However, any chargeable premiums may be covered by the various exemptions or by the nil rate band.

For a husband and wife the policy can be written on a joint lives, first death or surviving spouse basis. If the bulk of the estate is to be left to the spouse the tax charge will arise on the death of the surviving spouse. By taking out a joint life surviving spouse policy, the premiums will continue to be paid by the surviving spouse but the policy will not mature until the second death. The premiums payable are normally cheaper than a single life policy.

Annual premium of a with profit minimum cost whole life policy written on a joint life surviving spouse basis.

Age of husband next birthday	Age of wife next birthday	Sum assured £100,000 Annual premium
		£
30	26	151
40	36	285
50	46	586
60	56	1,221

The above quotes are on the basis that the assured are non-smokers.

The problem which both donor and donee face when a potentially exempt lifetime gift is made is that it is not known at that time whether the gift will escape IHT, as gifts made within seven years of death are caught. The example in the section which covered the cumulation period showed that a gift of £120,000 made four and a half years before death would attract a tax charge of £2,400 and the estate would suffer additional tax of £44,000, a total of £46,400. If the entire estate is to pass to, say, the son, he will be as concerned as the donor over this matter and may wish to ensure that any additional tax in the event of the donor's death is covered by the maturity of a life assurance policy. Due to tapering relief the tax charge will fall if death occurs between three and seven years after making the gift.

A special term assurance policy called an inter-vivos assurance policy can provide for the additional tax charge. The policy could be taken out by the donor with the proceeds of the policy passing to the beneficiaries. In this case the premiums will be chargeable transfers if death occurs within seven years. If the donor survives seven years the policy will lapse and no further premiums will be required.

An individual with an estate of £450,000 wishes to gift £150,000 and protect against the additional tax if he dies within seven years.

No. of years between gift and death	Additional tax charge
	£
0—3	60,000
3—4	56,800
4—5	53,600
5—6	50,400
6—7	47,200
7—8	Nil

Cost of 'inter-vivos' assurance premium for seven years to cover the above tax

Man aged	Annual premium
	£
30	130
40	180
50	360
60	835

The single premium bond

The use of a single premium bond in estate planning became popular under CTT legislation as part of the inheritance trust arrangement. Often the donor wanted to gift while still having the ability to take back the value of the bond if he so wished. This opportunity to 'have your cake and eat it' has now been seriously curtailed by the gifts with reservation rules. However, the basic interest-free loan arrangement can still work under the IHT regime. You lend funds, on an interest-free basis to the beneficiaries while retaining a form of annual income in the form of loan repayments. The growth in the funds will accrue to your beneficiaries outside your estate and so escape IHT. The same objective could be achieved by utilising a Trust and making a loan to the trustees on the same basis.

Clearly, any benefit from these arrangements will depend upon the success of the insurance company in managing the funds within the bond. It is possible, if the investment is badly managed, for the value of the bond to be less than the loan due to the estate. The single premium bond could be invested in secure funds, such as a UK money market fund, so that this risk is avoided. A similar arrangement can be devised using gilts instead of a single premium bond and the 'income requirement' can be a fluctuating figure.

The steps involved are as follows:

1) an interest-free loan, repayable on demand, is made to your beneficiaries or to a trust for their benefit;

2) the beneficiaries, or trustees, use the money to buy a single premium bond;

3) irregular partial surrenders may be made from the bond. This is used to repay part of the loan so that the lender receives 'annual income';

4) on the death of the lender, any outstanding loan must be repaid.

Any profit arising upon encashment of the single premium bond attracts income tax at the higher (not the basic) rates subject to top slicing relief. An income tax charge may be avoided if the annual partial surrender is less than 5%, any excess over 5% will be chargeable. These partial surrenders to produce 'income' could continue for 20 years without incurring an income tax charge. It is important to avoid the Inland Revenue claiming that the repayments are income and therefore regular withdrawals and repayments should be avoided.

An individual who is a 40% taxpayer with an estate of £500,000, has £100,000 invested in the money market producing 10% gross income p.a. He lends £100,000 to his son who will inherit his estate and who acquires a single premium bond and repays the loan by 5% partial surrenders for five years until his father dies when the bond is worth £150,000.

	£	£	£
Lender			
Income from money market			10,000
Less Tax at 40%			(4,000)
Net income			6,000
'Income' from loan repayment			5,000
Reduction in 'income'			1,000
Son			
Original investment			100,000
Less IHT at 40%			40,000
			60,000
Funds from repayment of loan		75,000	
Less IHT at 40%		(30,000)	
Net funds passing on death		45,000	
Encashment of bond	150,000		
Less Income tax	(11,250)		
Loan repayment	(75,000)		
Net value		63,750	
			108,750
Benefit			£48,750

Gilts and endowment policies

A similar estate planning exercise can be carried out using a series of gilts and a number of endowment policies. The steps involved are as follows:

a) A number of gilts with different maturity dates are acquired. They are selected so that they mature in consecutive years.

b) A series of endowment policies are taken out and assigned in trust for the children.

c) Each year one of the gilts will mature to provide tax-free capital appreciation. Income is also received from the gilts. These funds are used to pay any tax on the income from the gilts and the annual premium on the endowment policies. The balance is used to provide 'income' as required.

The arrangement can be implemented by the investor or by his beneficiaries, in which case an interest-free loan will be made by the investor and his 'annual income' will be received by a partial repayment of the loan. Again this should be irregular.

The gilts can be high income producing if the recipient pays tax at the lower rates, or geared to produce tax-free capital appreciation if the investor is a higher rate taxpayer. If the endowment policy is held for ten years (in some cases this can be seven and a half years) any profit on encashment will not be subject to income tax. The arrangement can provide the lender with fluctuating 'income' if his income pattern and future requirements can be determined.

A similar exercise can be effected by using an annuity or an investment trust instead of gilts.

An individual is a 40% taxpayer with £100,000 currently invested on the money market. He is 63 years of age and his wife is 57. He uses the funds to invest in the gilt/endowment plan. The policy is written in trust for his children, the premiums on which are covered by his annual exemptions. He dies ten years after taking out the plan.

Current net spendable income

	£
Interest from money market at, say, 10%	10,000
Less Tax	(4,000)
	6,000
Income under gilt plan	(5,000)
Decrease in net spendable income	1,000
Conservative estimate of policies passing free of IHT to his children	131,000

If the investor does not wish to loan the money to his dependants to enable them to invest in the gilt/endowment plan and does not wish to lose control of his investment from the outset, he could set up the plan and decide each year how many policies he wishes to gift.

Annuities

An annuity is a lump sum investment with a life insurance company which will produce a regular guaranteed level of income, which can be index-linked or unit-linked.

The investment can be made on a joint life basis so that the payments are made during the life of both husband and wife. Part of the payment is treated as a repayment of capital and is not taxable. The balance is deemed to be income and is subject to income tax. On death the payments cease and no capital is returned to the estate unless a capital protection policy is taken out which guarantees a payment of an amount at least equal to the cost of the investment. Most companies offer some form of guarantee such as a five year pay back period.

The annuity plan is suitable for elderly investors who need to maximise their after tax income and do not mind reducing the wealth they pass to their beneficiaries. A disadvantage of this form of arrangement is that, once taken out, it is usually not possible to surrender the annuity. It is possible that supplementary benefits and the age allowance may be adversely affected.

Annuity payable on an investment of £100,000 to a 40% income taxpayer

	Annuity net of 40% tax	
Age	*Male*	*Female*
	£	£
50	8,016	7,524
60	9,456	8,544
65	10,548	9,372
70	11,976	10,524

The above rates were quoted on 25 August 1988.

The major part of an estate can be the value of the home and often an elderly house owner will have repaid his mortgage. The property value can be partially unlocked by a taxpayer who is at least 70 years old (normally married couples must have combined ages of 150 years), borrowing up to £30,000 against the value of the home. In these circumstances the interest payable on the mortgage will attract income tax relief so long as at least 90% of the loan is used to purchase an annuity. The mortgage will be a debt on the estate which can be repaid out of the proceeds from the house. However, in the past these arrangements have not been popular as the annuity rates have been relatively poor.

Overseas planning

Generally

At the time of publication of this book a consultative document on overseas taxation had been published. The following is based upon current tax practice which may change if certain of the proposals of the consultative documents are enacted as mentioned later in this chapter. While most people may be familiar with the general rules relating to residence and ordinary residence for income tax and capital gains tax purposes, the term domicile may not be fully understood. IHT is geared to a person's domicile rather than his residence; the two following principles govern the scope of the tax.

1) IHT is chargeable on all the assets of a person domiciled in the UK, wherever they may be situated; and

2) IHT is chargeable on all the assets situated in the UK regardless of where the person who owns the assets is domiciled.

Therefore, if you are not domiciled in the UK you can escape IHT if you transfer your property outside the UK. As no exchange control regulations are currently in force, this is an ideal time for a non-UK domiciled person to consider IHT planning which may, in any case, require urgent action for various reasons which will be considered later in this book.

Often the opportunity to take advantage of not being domiciled in the UK for income, capital gains and IHT purposes is overlooked. An individual may move to the UK and recognise that he will become resident in the UK and so will need to complete a tax return. There is a special form which should be used by non-domiciled persons. However, if a normal return is filed, the Inland Revenue will assume that he is both resident and domiciled in the UK. It may be more difficult, several years later, if the individual becomes aware that he could have claimed to be non-domiciled in the UK for him to then obtain a favourable ruling.

Domicile

The term domicile is a matter of general law and is crucial in the context of IHT. Its rules are different from those of residence and it should not be confused with nationality. Under English law everyone has a domicile. Unlike residence which mainly depends upon where you are living at a particular point in time, domicile broadly speaking, depends upon where you consider your true home to be. A person may for example be born in France and have lived in the UK for several years but intend to return to France and spend the rest of his life there. In these circumstances, he is likely to be domiciled in France but resident (and possibly ordinarily resident) in the UK.

When an individual is born, he acquires a domicile of origin which is usually his father's domicile (unless the child is illegitimate or born after the father's death in which case the child will take the mother's domicile). The child's domicile will follow that of his father but at the age of 16 (or earlier upon marriage) he may acquire a domicile of choice if he moves to another country with a view to settling there permanently.

A woman married before 1 January 1974 takes her husband's domicile unless she abandons it by actions of her own (e.g. she has settled permanently in another country) but a woman who married after 31 December 1973 can have a domicile which is different from that of her husband. For example the husband may have a UK domicile but his wife, who was born and lived in the US until her marriage, may have moved to the UK. If both she and her husband intend to settle in the US ultimately, she may not be domiciled in the UK.

Special rules apply if a person who is not domiciled in the UK has been resident in the UK for seventeen of the last twenty years of assessment or if he was domiciled in the UK in the last three years before a chargeable transfer. In these circumstances, he will be deemed to be domiciled in the UK. Urgent action may therefore be required to protect the estate if a person will shortly be deemed domiciled in the UK.

The Inland Revenue has ruled an individual is not domiciled in the UK but he has been UK resident for a number of years. He will become deemed UK domiciled as follows:

Fiscal year in which he first became UK resident	*Date on which he is deemed to become domiciled in the UK*
1972/73	6 April 1988
1973/74	6 April 1989
1974/75	6 April 1990
1975/76	6 April 1991

As mentioned earlier, the Government is presently reviewing the system of income and capital taxation as applied to non-resident and/or non-UK domiciled taxpayers. Whilst the current proposals do not directly affect inheritance tax, there are indications that the deemed domicile rules may change. For instance, the relevant period may be shortened from seventeen out of twenty years to seven out of fourteen years.

A non-UK domiciled individual who is not ordinarily resident has a house in the UK worth £200,000, UK investments of £150,000 and UK property worth £100,000. He sells his investments and property and reinvests the money in UK gilts and foreign property.

	£000	£
Original UK estate	450	
IHT thereon		136,000
Revised position (ignoring any CGT charge)		
UK gilts (excluded property)	150	
Overseas property (excluded property)	100	
	250	
House (chargeable property)	200	
	450	
IHT on chargeable property		36,000
IHT saving		£100,000

Excluded property

A person who is not domiciled in the UK may still have assets in this country, even after he has emigrated from the UK. If he dies, those UK assets will be subject to IHT. By rearranging his wealth so that excluded rather than chargeable assets are held, substantial savings can be made. Excluded property includes property situated abroad and certain UK government stock.

The use of trusts

If a person is likely to become deemed UK domiciled, the potential IHT charge may be mitigated by transferring assets situated abroad into a trust. This is because settled property which is situated abroad is excluded property if the settlor was domiciled outside the UK when he formed the settlement. Therefore the property within the trust may be protected even if the settlor acquires a UK domicile for IHT purposes. It may be advisable to ensure that the property in the trust is passed to the children on the death of the settlor, because if it passes to the wife who is then domiciled in the UK it can revert to being chargeable property.

The settlor may wish to spread his wealth so that part of it is outside the UK. At present, there are no exchange control restrictions and it is very unlikely that foreign settled property would need to be repatriated even if exchange controls were to be reintroduced.

No capital gains tax arises on gifting assets such as gilts, building society deposits and bank deposits etc. to a non-resident trust. The transfer of other assets into a non-resident trust can have adverse capital gains tax implications which will need to be considered. If the value of the asset e.g. shares in the family company, is much greater than its original cost, a capital gain may arise on the transfer. If the asset is gifted to a UK settlement for the settlor or his family, the gain can be 'held over' so that tax is only payable when the asset is sold by the trust. However, the transfer of an asset to a non-resident trust will crystallise the tax charge and the gain cannot be 'held over'. Additionally, if a UK trust becomes non-resident (by the appointment of non-resident trustees), any gain which has been 'held over' will become chargeable. The use of a special class of shares in this situation may be appropriate.

Although a capital gains tax charge could arise on gifting shares in the family company to an overseas trust this may not deter the settlor if the shares are likely to increase in value (possibly because the company will be going to the USM in the next few years), as any tax charge on the future growth in the value of the shares could be deferred and also cash may shortly be available to pay the immediate tax charge.

Funds invested in an overseas trust may generate capital gains which if made by a UK resident would be taxable. These gains will accumulate tax-free until the trust distributes capital to its UK beneficiaries. Again, this planning opportunity may be curtailed if legislation is introduced following the proposed wide review of the taxation treatment of offshore trusts.

The income tax position of the overseas trust depends upon the status of the beneficiaries. If the settlor or his wife has an interest in the trust, the UK income will be treated as his and will be subject to UK income tax at the full rates. However, if the trust is an accumulation and maintenance settlement for his minor children the UK source income may be subject to tax at 35%. By transferring the assets of the trust to a wholly owned non-resident company, this tax charge can be reduced to the basic rate of 25%. Further tax may be payable when income is paid out of the trust but such payments may be deferred for many years.

Double tax treaties

In any case where a non-resident or non-UK domiciled person is involved or the estate includes overseas assets or there is a non-resident trust, the effect of overseas taxes must be taken into account at the planning stage.

This may require a careful examination of the domestic tax legislation of the relevant country and any double taxation treaties.

Capital gains tax

Generally

Capital gains tax often requires careful consideration during an estate planning exercise. Income tax considerations may also need to be taken into account but these may not be an overriding factor. A gift of cash, building society deposits or bank deposit funds will not be subject to capital gains tax but a gift of shares or property could give rise to a tax charge if the value of the asset exceeds the total of its base cost, the indexation allowance and any available annual exemption. (The provisions of the Finance Act 1988 now allow the market value of the asset as at 31 March 1982 to form the base cost in certain circumstances.) If the capital gains tax is paid by the donee it can be deducted from the chargeable transfer for IHT purposes.

A widow with an income of £25,000 p.a. gives shares worth £150,000 in a quoted company to her son. They cost her £60,000 in March 1982. She has not utilised her annual capital gains tax exemption.

	£
Value of gift	150,000
March 1982 value	(60,000)
	90,000
Indexation allowance £60,000 ×, say, 35%	(21,000)
	69,000
Annual exemption	(5,000)
Chargeable gain	£64,000
Capital gains tax £64,000 × 40%	£25,600

Deferring capital gains tax

Although a gift may create a capital gain it is possible to 'hold over' the gain if an election is made within six years from the end of the year of assessment in which the gain arises. The election may be made in the following cases:

— A gift by an individual to another UK resident individual

— A gift by an individual to UK resident trustees

— A gift from one UK resident trust to another or to a UK resident individual

The election in respect of the gift between two individuals requires the signature of both parties whereas an election in respect of a gift by an individual to a trust only requires the donor's signature. No election can be made if the gift is to a non-resident individual or trust. Also the emigration of the transferee can crystallise the gain originally 'held over'.

As a result of an election any chargeable gain arising from the gift is 'held over' so that no tax is payable at that time. If the recipient himself makes a gift of the asset a further election can be made to defer the charge so that tax is only payable when the asset is ultimately sold. The base cost of the asset in the transferee's hands will be the value of the property when the gift was made less any chargeable gain that was then held over. If cash is paid for the asset so that there is a partial gift and partial sale the held over gain is reduced by the excess of the consideration over the base cost of the asset.

Facts as in the previous example but the widow dies four and a half years after making the gift. Six months later, the son sells the shares for £200,000.

	£	£
Estate		
IHT payable on gift		£9,600
Son's deemed acquisition cost		
Value of gift		150,000
Less Held over gain		(69,000)
		£81,000
Tax charge on son		
Proceeds from sale of shares		200,000
Base cost (as above)	81,000	
IHT borne by son, as above	9,600	
Further indexation from the date of gift to date of sale £81,000 ×, say, 20%	16,200	(106,000)
		93,200
Annual exemption, say		(5,000)
Chargeable gain		88,200
Capital gains tax at, say, 40%		£35,280

If any IHT is payable on the gift, possibly because it is a gift to a trust or a gift to an individual which is made within seven years of the donor's death, the tax payable is deducted from the chargeable gain arising.

Position on death

Any capital losses arising in the year of death can be carried back three years. All assets held by an individual at the time of his death are deemed to be acquired by his personal representatives at their then market value. Therefore the base cost of an asset for capital gains tax purposes is revised to market value. If the personal representatives or the beneficiaries then sell the asset a tax charge may arise on any appreciation in value since the donor's death.

A widow has assets worth £450,000 and gifts an asset worth £100,000 to her son in June 1988, more than seven years before her death. It cost £40,000 in 1982 and is worth £150,000 on her death at which time her son sells it for that amount.

	£
Capital gains tax charge on son	
Proceeds	150,000
Less Base cost (£40,000 plus indexation to date of gift, say, £12,000)	(52,000)
	98,000
Less Indexation from date of gift £52,000 × 40%	(20,800)
	77,200
Less Annual capital gains tax exemption (say)	(5,000)
Chargeable gain	£72,200
Capital gains tax at, say, 40%	£28,880
If the asset had been left to the son on death and sold for £150,000 at that time the position would be	
Capital gains tax	Nil
Additional IHT on estate £150,000 × 40%	60,000
	£60,000
Net benefit from gift	£31,120

As capital gains tax can be avoided or substantially reduced by bequeathing an asset on death rather than gifting it during lifetime, this can produce a dilemma; it will be necessary to weigh up the potential IHT savings against the additional capital gains tax which may ultimately be payable when an asset is sold. The following example shows that a lifetime gift made more than seven years before death would be beneficial even after the capital gains tax charge. However, the position could be reversed if death occurs shortly after making the gift since the recipient would not benefit from the free uplift to market value on death.

Retirement relief

This is a very important form of capital gains tax relief which may apply on a sale or gift of shares in the family trading company (or of the whole or part of a business) by an individual who is 60 years of age (or younger than 60 if he has retired on grounds of ill health).

The rules broadly require that the business or shares must have been held by the donor for a complete year before the gift. If the conditions for relief have been fulfilled during the previous ten years, the first £125,000 of gains will be exempt together with half of any further gains between £125,000 and £500,000. Where the conditions have been fulfilled for more than one year but less than ten years the relief is scaled down. It is a condition that the donor was a full-time working director throughout the period and the shares gifted must relate to a family trading company. This means that of the voting rights:

1) at least 25% were exercisable by the donor; or

2) at least 5% were exercisable by the donor and over 50% were exercisable by his family.

It is possible to look through a trust if the beneficiaries are members of the family for this purpose. (Family includes the spouse and a relative of the donor or his spouse — relative means brother, sister, ancestor or lineal descendant.) A reduction in relief may be made if the company or business owns non-business assets.

If some shares are to be gifted while others are to be sold it may be advisable to ensure that the relief is given when it is most needed and this will probably be on the sale as the gain on a gift could be 'held over'. It may therefore be necessary to time the transactions so that the sale occurs before the gift.

For estate planning purposes it may be advisable for a husband to gift shares in the family company to his wife, but if she is not a full-time working director of the company no retirement relief will be due when she sells or gifts the shares during her lifetime.

The share capital of a company is owned as follows:

	No. of shares	%
A	2,500	25
B	2,500	25
C	2,500	25
D	2,500	25
	10,000	100

None of the shareholders are related to each other.

If A gifts 1,000 shares to his son now and the remaining 1,500 shares in a year, retirement relief would be available on the first transfer but not on the second.

If A gifts all his shares to his son now the entire transfer would qualify for relief.

Utilising the annual capital gains tax exemption

The annual capital gains tax exemption is currently £5,000. Everyone has an annual exemption but it is lost if it is not utilised each year. At present, married couples share the exemption although if one spouse has available capital losses these could be used against that spouse's gains leaving the gains of the other spouse to be covered by the annual exemption. From 1990/91, each spouse will have their own annual exemption. Children have their own exemption whatever their age. The exemption for a trust is normally half of an individual's exemption, i.e. £2,500.

If a taxpayer who normally utilises his annual exemption each year, wishes to carry out an estate planning exercise, he could gift assets which are likely to be sold in due course at a gain. For example, he could gift an asset to his children, make an election to 'hold over' the gain which would be chargeable on the children when the assets are sold but may be covered by their annual exemption. Anti-avoidance provisions could apply to this arrangement but if the gift is clearly made well before the sale was contemplated and if the net proceeds are retained by the donees, such provisions should not apply.

Converting a deferral into an exemption

This could be effected by gifting an investment property to a donee who will use it as his principal private residence. An election can be made to 'hold over' the capital gain, but no tax will be payable by the donee on a sale of the property if it has been used as his home throughout his period of ownership.

An individual who has three young children, has 3,000 shares in a company. They are worth £27,000, cost £9,000 and the indexation allowance to date is £3,000. He normally uses his annual capital gains tax exemption.

	£	£
If he sells the shares		
Proceeds		27,000
Cost	(9,000)	
Indexation allowance	(3,000)	
		(12,000)
Chargeable gain		15,000
CGT at 40%		£6,000
If he gifts 1,000 shares to each child who then sells the shares		
Proceeds per child		9,000
Less £12,000 divided by 3		(4,000)
		5,000
Annual exemption		(5,000)

There would be no capital gains tax payable

Payment and administration of IHT

Administration

Broadly speaking, the persons who will be liable for the tax will include the transferor, the beneficiary of the gift, personal representatives and the trustees and beneficiaries of a trust to which property is transferred. An account must be submitted to the Inland Revenue normally within twelve months of death or of the chargeable transfer. Under the IHT regime the donee will be required to submit an account within twelve months of the death of the donor in respect of a gift (including a gift with reservation) to him which is caught because it was made within seven years of death. An appeal against an IHT determination must be made in writing within 30 days.

Payment of tax

The due dates for payment of IHT are set out below.

Event	Payment date
Chargeable transfer during lifetime (e.g. gift to a discretionary trust)	
— Between 6 April and 30 September	Following 30 April
— Between 1 October and 5 April	6 months after month of transfer
Death (including additional tax on potentially exempt lifetime or chargeable transfer within seven years of death)	6 months after month of death
Certain other chargeable events (e.g. sale of woodlands)	6 months after month of event

If the personal representatives borrow to enable the IHT to be paid before the grant of representation or confirmation, tax relief should be available on the loan interest for a period of twelve months after the loan is made.

Payment by instalments

If on the death of the donor IHT is payable in respect of the following assets the tax may, if an election is made, be paid by ten equal annual instalments starting from six months from the date of death or from the normal payment date.

The qualifying assets are:

1) land;

2) shares of a company in which the transferor, deceased or trustee had control;

3) unquoted shares if the chargeable event is the death of the donor and at least 20% of the tax payable relates to such shares or the other assets in respect of which tax can be paid by instalments;

4) unquoted shares if payment of tax in full would give rise to hardship;

5) unquoted shares worth at least £20,000 if their nominal value represents more than 10% of the total nominal value;

6) a business or an interest in a business.

If the charge arises on a potentially exempt transfer which becomes chargeable because of the donor's death within seven years, the relevant asset must still be held by the donee for the instalment method to be claimed. Any outstanding interest on overdue instalments is added to the next instalment due. If the relevant property is sold the outstanding tax (and interest) is payable immediately. The outstanding instalments may be paid at any time if so preferred.

Woodlands are afforded special treatment. It may be that the tax which is due in respect of woodlands has been deferred and becomes payable due to a disposal of the woodlands. If the disposal is itself a chargeable transfer the person paying the tax may elect to pay by instalments. The deferred tax must in any event be paid six months after the end of the month in which the disposal was made.

Interest on unpaid tax

If tax is not paid on the due date, interest on unpaid tax (which is not an allowable deduction for tax purposes) is charged as set out below.

Event	*Rate of interest*
	%
Chargeable transfer on death	9
Potentially exempt transfer which becomes chargeable because of the donor's death within seven years	9
Any other case	10.75
These rates were correct as at 30 November 1988.	

Penalties

The following offences carry penalties as set out below.

		Penalty not exceeding
Failure to deliver an account	—	£50, and, if failure continues after declaration by a court or the Special Commissioners, £10 per day.
Failure to make a return	—	as above.
Failure to comply with a notice	—	as above.
Failure to appear before Special Commissioners	—	£50.
Provision of incorrect information	—	if fraudulent and person liable for the tax, £50 plus twice the additional tax due.
	—	if fraudulent and person not liable for the tax, £500.
	—	if negligent and person liable for the tax £50, plus the additional tax due.
	—	if negligent and person not liable for the tax, £250.
	—	if assisting or inducing an incorrect return, £500.

There are provisions for the Board to mitigate any penalty at their discretion.

Appendix 1

Inheritance tax rates 1988/89

Chargeable transfer	Rate of tax
£000	%
0—110	Nil
over 110	40

Inheritance tax grossing up rates 1988/89

Transfer more than seven years before death

Chargeable transfer	Rate of tax
£	
0—110,000	Nil
over 110,000	¼ (25.00%)

Transfer within seven years of death

Chargeable transfer	Rate of tax
£	
0—110,000	Nil
over 110,000	⅔ (66.67%)

Appendix 2

Estimated capital and income

	Capital		Gross income	
	Self	*Spouse*	*Self*	*Spouse*
	£000	*£000*	*£*	*£*
Assets				
Private residence		220	4,800	—
Other property	80		4,800	—
Shares in the trading company		360		
Bank deposit accounts	30		3,000	
Building society deposits	40	60	4,000	6,000
Shares in quoted companies	50		3,000	
Gilts and other securities		60		1,900
	560	340	14,800	7,900
Remuneration			45,000	
Benefits			3,000	
Liabilities				
Mortgage on house		(30)		(3,900)
Other property loans	(40)		(4,800)	
Tax and other liabilities	(20)			
	500	310	58,000	4,000
Life policies — sum assured	100		—	
Value of pension schemes	500		—	

Appendix 3

Estimated capital statement

<table>
<tr><td></td><td colspan="4" align="center">Assets and liabilities at current values</td></tr>
<tr><td></td><td colspan="2" align="center">Self</td><td colspan="2" align="center">Spouse</td></tr>
<tr><td></td><td>£000</td><td>£000</td><td>£000</td><td>£000</td></tr>
<tr><td>Home</td><td></td><td></td><td></td><td></td></tr>
<tr><td>Principal residence</td><td></td><td></td><td></td><td>220</td></tr>
<tr><td>Less Mortgage</td><td></td><td></td><td></td><td>(30)</td></tr>
<tr><td></td><td></td><td></td><td></td><td>190</td></tr>
<tr><td>Investment Property</td><td></td><td></td><td></td><td></td></tr>
<tr><td>Other property</td><td>80</td><td></td><td></td><td></td></tr>
<tr><td>Less Loans</td><td>(40)</td><td></td><td></td><td></td></tr>
<tr><td></td><td></td><td>40</td><td></td><td></td></tr>
<tr><td>Unquoted shares</td><td></td><td></td><td></td><td></td></tr>
<tr><td>Shares in the trading company</td><td></td><td></td><td>360</td><td></td></tr>
<tr><td>Investments</td><td></td><td></td><td></td><td></td></tr>
<tr><td>Bank deposit accounts</td><td>30</td><td></td><td></td><td></td></tr>
<tr><td>Building society deposits</td><td>40</td><td></td><td>60</td><td></td></tr>
<tr><td>Shares in quoted companies</td><td>50</td><td></td><td></td><td></td></tr>
<tr><td>Gilts and other securities</td><td>—</td><td></td><td>60</td><td></td></tr>
<tr><td></td><td>120</td><td></td><td>120</td><td></td></tr>
<tr><td>Less Tax and other liabilities</td><td>(20)</td><td></td><td>—</td><td></td></tr>
<tr><td></td><td></td><td>100</td><td></td><td>120</td></tr>
<tr><td></td><td></td><td>500</td><td></td><td>310</td></tr>
<tr><td>Life policies — sum assured</td><td></td><td>100</td><td></td><td></td></tr>
<tr><td>Pension scheme (likely
  tax-free cash £60,000)</td><td></td><td>500</td><td></td><td></td></tr>
</table>

Appendix 4

Estimated IHT calculation

Assuming — all assets to be left to spouse on first death and husband dies first

— mortgage repaid on death by redemption of endowment policy

— shares in trading company sold by wife immediately after his death

— tax-free cash sum of £60,000 due from pension fund, balance used to produce the annual pension

	£	£
Net assets — self		500,000
— spouse		310,000
Add Mortgage repaid on death of husband		30,000
Proceeds from life policy		100,000
Likely tax-free cash sum from pension		60,000
		1,000,000
IHT — on £110,000	Nil	
£890,000 × 40%	356,000	
1,000,000		(356,000)
Net estate after IHT		£644,000

Appendix 5

Estimated net spendable income summary 1988/89

	Taxable income		Net spendable income
	£	£	£
Remuneration from trading company		45,000	45,000
Benefits in kind		3,000	
		48,000	
Investment income			
Property income	4,800		
Less Loan interest	(4,800)		
	—		
Bank deposit interest (Self)	3,000		
Building society interest (Both)		10,000	
Dividends (Self)	3,000		
Income from gilts (Wife)	1,900		
	17,900		
Less Mortgage interest	(3,900)		
		14,000	14,000
		62,000	59,000
Less Personal allowance		(4,095)	
Taxable income		57,905	
Tax thereon: £19,300 × 25%		4,825	
38,605 × 40%		15,442	
57,905		£20,267	(20,267)
Net spendable income			38,733
Annual expenditure			(35,000)
Surplus income			£3,733

Appendix 6

Likely items of annual expenditure

—   General rates/community charge
—   Water rates
—   Rent
—   Gas
—   Electricity
—   Telephone
—   House repairs and improvements
—   Insurance — home, car, permanent health etc
—   Mortgage interest/repayments
—   Other loan interest
—   Maintenance payments
—   Holidays
—   Subscriptions (golf club, church etc)
—   Charitable donations
—   Clothes
—   Car expenses, petrol etc
—   Doctor's fees
—   School fees
—   Food bills
—   Spending money, entertainment etc

Appendix 7

Likely income after husband's death

Likely income producing capital

	£000	£000
Investment property less loan		40
Net investments — husband	100	
— wife	120	
		220
Proceeds from life policy		100
Tax-free cash sum from pension scheme		60
Available funds producing gross income of, say, 10% p.a.		420

Likely income	*Taxable income*	*Net spendable income*
	£	£
£420,000 × 10%	42,000	42,000
Personal allowance	(2,605)	
Taxable income	39,395	
Tax thereon: £19,300 × 25%	4,825	
20,095 × 40%	8,038	
39,395		(12,863)
Net spendable income		29,137
Annual expenditure (say)		25,000
Surplus income		£4,137

Further considerations — income from or sale of shares in family trading company

                          — pension from state or company scheme

Appendix 8

Brief summary of certain leading estate duty cases

Munro-v-Commissioner of Stamp Duty (1934)

This case held that gifts with reservation rules did not apply to an interest which was 'carved out' before a gift was made. The taxpayer carried on the business of a grazier on 35,000 acres of land. He verbally entered into a partnership agreement with his children in respect of the business which was to continue to be managed solely by him. Four years later he gifted the land to his children. It was held that the gift was the land shorn of the rights belonging to the partnership.

Nichols-v-IRC (1975)

A property was gifted by a father to his son with a simultaneous leaseback. It was held that duty was chargeable on the unencumbered property and not the property shorn of the lease.

Chick-v-Commissioners of Stamp Duties (1958)

The taxpayer gave his son land outright and seventeen months later entered into a partnership agreement with him for the use of the land. The father was the manager of the business. It was held that the gifts with reservation rules should apply.

Commissioner of Stamp Duties of NS Wales-v-Permanent Trustee Co (1956)

In 1924 a property was transferred by a taxpayer to a trust for his daughter's benefit. In 1940 the father received money from the trust. It was held that the gifts with reservation rules applied to the entire trust fund.

Attorney General-v-Worral (1895)

This case held that a gift in return for an annuity under covenant was fully chargeable.

Re Cochrane (1906)

The taxpayer settled £15,000 on trust under which a set amount of income was payable to his daughter with the balance to the settlor. The full amount settled was held to be chargeable.

Grey (Earl)-v-Attorney General (1900)

A gift was made subject to the taxpayer receiving an annual rent charge, the use of the property and certain other benefits. The gift was held to be a gift with reservation.

Oakes-v-Commissioner of Stamp Duties of NS Wales (1954)

A gift subject to the donor receiving reasonable remuneration as a manager of the property was held to be a benefit and this decision could be relevant to a gift of shares in a family company.

Commissioner of Stamp Duties of NS Wales-v-Perpetual Trustee Co Ltd (1943)

This held that the settlor may be one of the trustees without the gifts with reservation rules applying.

Appendix 9

Potential IHT savings on lifetime transfers

Value of estate before gift	Potential reduction in tax on lifetime transfer made more than seven years before death				
£000	Gift of £50,000	Gift of £100,000	Gift of £150,000	Gift of £200,000	Gift of £250,000
150,000	16,000	16,000	16,000	N/A	N/A
200,000	20,000	36,000	36,000	36,000	N/A
250,000	20,000	40,000	56,000	56,000	56,000
300,000	20,000	40,000	60,000	76,000	76,000
400,000 and above	20,000	40,000	60,000	80,000	100,000

Appendix 10

Business property relief and agricultural property relief

Business property relief

The business carried on by the company must not consist wholly or mainly of one or more of the following

1) dealing in securities;

2) dealing in stocks or shares;

3) dealing in land or buildings;

4) making or holding investments.

Agricultural property relief

Agricultural property means 'agricultural land or pasture and includes woodland and any building used in connection with the intensive rearing of livestock or fish if the woodland or building is occupied with agricultural land or pasture and the occupation is ancillary to that of the agricultural land or pasture; and also includes such cottages, farm buildings and farm-houses, together with the land occupied with them, as are of a character appropriate to the property'.

The breeding and rearing of horses on a stud farm and the grazing of horses in connection with those activities shall be taken to be agriculture and any buildings used in connection with those activities to be farm buildings.

If the property has been owned by the donor since 10 March 1981, the relevant conditions apply if in five of the previous seven years he had been carrying on a farming trade in the UK (or certain other permitted activities) and the property was occupied by him for the purposes of agriculture throughout the previous two years (or it replaced property which was so occupied during two of the last five years). Also since 10 March 1981 the property has not carried a right to vacant possession nor has it failed to do so by reason of an act of omission of the donor. Relief may be restricted if the appropriate relief as at 10 March 1981 was also restricted to 30% on the excess of the agricultural property over £250,000 or 1,000 acres.

Appendix 11

Intestacy rules under English law

Beneficiaries	Distribution of estate
Spouse but no children	First £125,000 and any personal possessions to spouse
	Balance — 50% to spouse
	—50% to parents (or brothers and sisters or nephews and nieces if parents dead)
	If no parents, brothers, sisters, nephews or nieces entire balance goes to spouse
Spouse and children	First £75,000 and any personal possessions to spouse
	Balance held on trust
	— 50% life interest for spouse
	— 50% for children
Children but no spouse	Estate divided equally among children
No spouse or children	Estate goes to the first of the following who are alive
	— parents
	— brothers and sisters
	— grandparents
	— aunts and uncles
	If there are no living relatives the estate will pass to the Crown

Appendix 12

Whole life assurance

With profits

The initial sum assured is increased by annual and terminal bonuses. The policy can normally be encashed after ten years and any profits will escape an income tax charge, otherwise a higher rate charge will arise subject to top slicing relief.

Without profit

The sum assured remains constant.

Low-cost

Combines a with profits whole life policy with a decreasing term assurance policy so that the sum assured will not increase as fast as the with profits policy but the premiums should be cheaper.

Unit linked

The sum assured is normally guaranteed for ten years and will thereafter reflect the value of the funds in which the premium is invested. The value of the policy will depend upon the performance of the funds. There are various forms of unit linked policies. Some have a minimum life cover and are more in the form of a savings plan. Others produce a standard cover under which the premiums should remain constant so long as the units appreciate at approximately 7.5% p.a. The maximum cover policies have a guaranteed sum assured but the premiums may need to be increased periodically depending upon the performance of the fund.

Inflation linked

The above policies can be inflation proof if the premiums increase in line with the retail prices index so that the sum assured and likely surrender value will be accordingly increased.

Appendix 13

Shareholding interests in a private company

Shareholding interest	Comments
£	
0—9	Only minority rights to avoid oppression from the majority shareholders
10—25	Their consent is required before an offer for the company can be declared unconditional
25—49	Can block a special or extraordinary resolution to say wind-up, sell the company or change its Articles of Association
50	Can block an ordinary resolution regarding normal business requirements such as appointment of directors. Could be the largest shareholder if the other shares are spread and so could control the company with the assistance of one other shareholder or in the absence of certain minority shareholders exercising their rights
51	Controls the company
75	Can pass a special or extraordinary resolution
90	Can accept an offer for shares in the company which will bind the other minority shareholders
100	Absolute control

Appendix 14

Independent taxation calculation

REVISED NET SPENDABLE INCOME SUMMARY 1988/89

	Taxable income		Net spendable income
	£	£	£
Self			
Remuneration from trading company		45,000	45,000
Benefits in kind		3,000	
		48,000	
Investment income			
Property income	4,800		
Less Loan interest	(4,800)		
	—		
Bank deposit interest	3,000		
Building society interest	4,000		
Dividends	3,000		
		10,000	10,000
		58,000	55,000
Less Allowances			
Personal	2,605		
Married couples	1,490		
		(4,095)	
Taxable income		53,905	
Tax thereon: £19,300 × 25%		4,825	
34,605 × 40%		13,842	
53,905		£18,667	(18,667)
Net spendable income			£36,333

Appendix 14 Continued

	Taxable income	Net *spendable income*
	£	£
Wife		
Investment income		
Building society	6,000	
Income from gilts	1,900	
	7,900	
Less Mortgage interest	(3,900)	
	4,000	4,000
Less Personal allowance	(2,605)	
Tax income	1,395	
Tax thereon: £1,395 × 25%	£349	(349)
Net spendable income		£3,651
Summary		
Tax payable/Net spendable income:		
Self	18,667	36,333
Wife	349	3,651
	19,016	39,984
Less Annual expenditure		(35,000)
		4,984
Tax payable/Net spendable income, per Appendix 5	(20,267)	(3,733)
Benefit	£(1,251)	£1,251

Index

Other Services of the firm

Accountancy & Audit

Accounting services

Computer bureau

Company secretarial

Financial planning

Specialised audits

Statutory audits

Financial Advice

Corporate finance and investigations

Entertainment industry

Litigation support

Mergers, acquisitions and flotations

Pensions planning

Personal financial planning

Property industry

Raising finance

Trust management

Venture capital

Insolvency

Administrations

Bankruptcy

Corporate rescue and reconstruction

Investigations

Liquidations

Receiverships

Voluntary arrangements

Consultancy Services

Business location

Corporate strategy

Design and selection of systems

Executive selection

Feasibility studies

Franchising services

Government grants

Hotel and leisure industries

Human resource services

Implementation of systems

Management training

Marketing studies

Organisation reviews

Project management

Urban regeneration advice

Tax

Business Expansion Scheme

Corporate taxation

International tax planning

Personal taxation

Remuneration/benefits planning

Tax investigations

UK tax planning

VAT & Customs Duty planning

Current publications

Client service brochures

Accounting Services (computer bureau)

Business Planning Services

Computers in Your Business

Executive Selection

Executive Tax Services

Foreign Trusts

Franchising

Going Bankrupt — Act Now!

Going Public

Human Resources

Insolvency Services

International Tax Services

Investment Monitoring Service

Legal Support Services

Management Consultancy Services

Micro Workshop

Personal Financial Planning

Profit Related Pay

Services to the Entertainment Industry

Services to the Property Industry

Stoy Hayward Review (annual)

Tax Investigations

Trustees and Trust Accountants

VAT & Customs Duty

Technical publications

Audit Guide £10.50

Business Expansion Scheme

Commentary on the Budget (annual)

CCH International Tax Planning Manual £250

Data Protection Act

Daily Telegraph Pensions Guide £10.95

HAC Guide to Taxation of the Bloodstock Industry £20

Model Financial Statements for public & private Cos £15.95

How to Franchise Your Business £7.95

Sources of Venture and Development Capital in the UK 1989 (annual)

The Stoy Hayward Business Tax Guide 1988/89 £14.95

Tax Data (annual)

Tax Planning Review (annual)

Surveys

A Study to Determine the Reasons for Failure of Small Businesses in the United Kingdom £20

Britain's Franchising Industry Survey (Jordans) £150

Corporate Venturing £25

The Essence of USM Success £40

Horwath & Horwath (UK) Publications

Horwath & Horwath (UK) Ltd Statement of Experience:
— Tourism, Hotel, Leisure and Related Industries
— Transportation
— Golf, Sports and Leisure
— Real Estate
— Tourist Attractions — Natural, historic and man made

An Examination of Tourism Incentives £10

World Tourism Organisation — Guidelines on Tourism Investment £10

Hotel & Tourism Insight £5

Hotel & Tourism Development £10

Tourism Multipliers Explained £10

United Kingdom Hotel Industry (annual) £25

Horwath & Horwath International — Worldwide Hotel Industry (annual) £30

United Kingdom offices

London

Stoy Hayward
Stoy Hayward Associates
Horwath & Horwath (UK) Ltd
8 Baker Street
London W1M 1DA
(01) 486 5888
Telex: 267716 HORWAT
Telefax: (Grps 3, 2 & 1)
(01) 487 3686
LDE Box No: DX 9025
Contact: Barry Stillerman

Aberdeen

Bower & Smith
30 Carden Place
Aberdeen AB9 1PQ
(0224) 638844
Contact: Nicol Geddes

Birmingham

Stoy Hayward
Pepper Rudland & Co.
Waterloo House
20 Waterloo Street
Birmingham B2 5TF
(021) 643 4024
Contact: Tony Supperstone

Bristol

Stoy Hayward
Solomon Hare
Oakfield House
Oakfield Grove
Clifton
Bristol BS8 2BN
(0272) 237000
Contact: Martin Brown

Glasgow

Stoy Hayward
McLachlan & Brown
James Sellars House
144 West George Street
Glasgow G2 2HG
(041) 331 2811
Contact: Jim Wylie

Leeds

Stoy Hayward
Thomas Coombs & Son
29 Clarendon Road
Leeds LS2 9PG
(0532) 449512
Contact: John Murtland

Manchester

Stoy Hayward
Elliott Templeton Sankey
Peter House
St Peter's Square
Manchester M1 5BH
(061) 228 6791
Contact: Grahame N Elliott

Norwich

Stoy Hayward
Hemming Graham & Poole
58 Thorpe Road
Norwich NR1 1RY
(0603) 660096
Contact: David Buck

Nottingham

Stoy Hayward
Phipp & Co.
Foxhall Lodge
Gregory Boulevard
Nottingham NG7 6LH
(0602) 626578
Contact: Alan Baines

Sunderland

Stoy Hayward
Jennings Johnson
19 Borough Road
Sunderland SR1 1LA
(091) 565 0565
Contact: Godfrey Jennings

International offices

Stoy Hayward is the UK member firm of Horwath & Horwath International and has 236 associated offices in the following countries:

Andorra
Argentina
Australia
Austria

Bahamas
Belgium
Bermuda
Bolivia
Brazil

Canada
Cayman Islands
Channel Islands
Chile
Colombia
Costa Rica

Denmark
Dominican
    Republic

Egypt
Ethiopia

Fiji
Finland
France

Germany
Greece
Guatemala

Haiti
Hong Kong
Hungary

Iceland
India
Indonesia
Ireland
Israel
Italy

Jamaica
Japan

Korea

Luxembourg

Malaysia
Mexico

Monaco
Morocco

Nepal
Netherlands
New Zealand
Nigeria
Norway

Pakistan
Panama
Peru
Portugal

Singapore
South Africa
Spain
Sri Lanka
Sweden
Switzerland
Syria

Taiwan
Thailand
Turkey

United States
Uruguay

Venezuela

Zimbabwe